Becoming Bilingual 1

Building on Bobbie Kabuto's groundbreaking 2010 book *Becoming Biliterate*, this book explores how identity impacts the development of bilingual readers and how reading practices are mediated by family and community contexts. Highlighting bilingual readers from Spanish, Greek, Japanese, and English language backgrounds, Kabuto offers an in-depth, interdisciplinary analysis of these readers' behaviors and identities through the original approach of Biographic Biliteracy Profiles.

The Profiles serve as a culturally relevant assessment tool for developing meaningful narratives and can reveal how bilingual readers make sense of texts in the context of their home and school environments. An ideal approach for unpacking the complexity of bilingual reading behaviors and how they change across time, the Profiles allow readers to explore what a bilingual reader's identity means to becoming biliterate; the roles of code-switching and translanguaging; the influences of readers' families and communities; and how they all interact and shape readers' identities, behaviors, and meaning-making.

Offering practical applications on observing and documenting bilingual readers, this book is an invaluable resource for scholars and students in courses on bilingualism, L2/ESL reading, and multilingualism.

Bobbie Kabuto is Professor of Literacy Education and Department Chair of the Elementary and Early Childhood Education Department at Queens College, City University of New York, USA.

Becoming Bilingual Readers

Identity, Translanguaging, and Biographic Biliteracy Profiles

Bobbie Kabuto

NEW YORK AND LONDON

First published 2022
by Routledge
605 Third Avenue, New York, NY 10158

and by Routledge
2 Park Square, Milton Park, Abingdon, Oxon, OX14 4RN

Routledge is an imprint of the Taylor & Francis Group, an informa business

Library of Congress Cataloging-in-Publication Data
A catalog record for this book has been requested

ISBN: 978-0-367-49392-9 (hbk)
ISBN: 978-0-367-49209-0 (pbk)
ISBN: 978-1-003-04598-4 (ebk)

DOI: 10.4324/9781003045984

Typeset in Bembo
by Apex CoVantage, LLC

To Denny

Contents

Figures/Tables

Figures

Tables

Acknowledgments

I would like to thank the many individuals who made this book possible. A special thank you goes to Thomas, Jenny, Mai, Sophie, and Emma. It has been an honor spending time with these thoughtful, engaging readers and their families who welcomed Livia, Despina, and me into their homes. In addition, this project would not have been possible without Livia Gama Fagundes and Despina Galatoulas, who spent many hours transcribing and translating the Spanish and Greek texts presented in this book. I was lucky to have you both.

I am indebted to my mentor and dear friend Denny Taylor for her ongoing support. The work in this book is dedicated to you because without your seminal and groundbreaking work in family literacy and Biographic Literacy Profiles, this book would not have been possible. And thank you to my editor Karen Adler at Routledge. Your thoughtful feedback helped me to work out the organization and ideas for the book.

I would like to give heartfelt and loving thank you to Luis Landivar. You have been there since the very beginning of this work and lent your ideas in many different ways. Most of all, when I was stuck, frustrated, or just being difficult, you always believed in me and reminded me to believe in myself.

(Re)Introduction to Becoming Biliterate

In 2003, I began my doctoral studies after spending three years in Tokyo, where I was a second grade and preschool teacher in two international schools. As part of my doctoral research, I conducted a parent research study of my daughter Emma's biliteracy from ages 3 to 7 years. Having lived across social, cultural, and linguistic borders – physically and metaphorically – and studying Emma's biliteracy as these borders merged or dissipated, I questioned not only what it means to conduct parent research as a process of inquiry (Kabuto & Martens, 2014) but also what it means to *become* biliterate, as I found it difficult to disconnect Emma's learning to navigate written language systems in English and Japanese from her evolving linguistic, social, and cultural identities at home and at school.

The year 2020 was the tenth anniversary of the publication of *Becoming Biliterate: Identity, Ideology, and Learning to Read and Write in Two Languages* (Kabuto, 2010). Emma is now 22 years old, and her journey of becoming biliterate continues. She eventually went on to study Japanese language at a university and majored in international affairs and economics, which led her to study at a university in Tokyo for one semester. As her journey continued, so did my understanding of the complexity of becoming biliterate.

Since the publication of *Becoming Biliterate*, I continually revisited Emma's data through the growing and expanding fields of bilingualism and biliteracy, sociolinguistics, and identity studies. The term *translanguaging* (Garcia & Wei, 2014) was only beginning to take shape when I was researching Emma's biliteracy and writing *Becoming Biliterate*. I recently conducted a search in an educational database for articles that included the keyword *translanguaging* published between 2000 and 2010. The search yielded 16 journal articles and six books. The same search between the dates of 2011 and 2019 yielded 1,403 journal articles and 18 books. This search does not include the growing dominance of the term that fills conference proceedings at the Literacy Research Association (LRA) and the American Educational Research Association (AERA).

With each article or book I read on translanguaging, I revisited my data on Emma, particularly the data I collected of her reading English and Japanese books between the ages of 3 and 7 years. As Sefton-Green and Rowsell

DOI: 10.4324/9781003045984-1

(2015) explained, revisiting involves returning to a research site or participants to "grapple with how the people they met again dealt with different perspectives in time, how stories from the past are mobilized in the present, and how future aspirations are imagined and enacted in talk" (p. 3). Through her longitudinal work with families, Compton-Lilly (2017) showed how revisiting research participants includes not only reconnecting with them in their current context but also going back to previously collected data to find new types of analyses that consider the nature of time and change in discourses. Consequently, revisiting studies have the potential to address the temporal nature of learning, literacy, identity, and how researchers grow and evolve as they return to data to look for patterns and new trajectories of investigation (Compton-Lilly, 2017).

In *Becoming Biliterate*, I discussed becoming biliterate through the dynamic use of named languages during reading and writing events from a code-switching perspective. Just as the identity of a person is dynamic, so is that of a field of study. The consequence of this identity-shifting is the evolving ways that we, as researchers, teachers, and scholars, talk about what it means to become biliterate as well as what that process and those behaviors look like. Researchers (e.g., Gort, 2006; Wei, 1999) who used a code-switching framework to discuss the language patterns of linguistically diverse children started to rethink the nature of language to challenge the idea that bilingualism means "two monolinguals in one" (Garcia, 2009). The shift from code-switching to translanguaging was predicated on the notion that language cannot be contained and limited to named languages. Code-switching (other scholars have used the terms code-mixing or code-meshing) was designed around the concept of named languages, and when these named languages (like Spanish and English) come into contact, something magical happens – speakers begin to create renewed language patterns within utterances in diverse and strategic ways. Developing various analytic lenses to observe code-switching, seminal researchers (Auer, 1999; Gumperz, 1982; Heller, 1988) examined how code-switching is indexical of social relationships and identities through "verbal action" (Auer, 1999). Code-switching created a body of work that connected language as symbolic to social identities (Blommaert & Verschueren, 1998) and how code-switching created shared frames of reference (Gumperz, 1982). From an analytic code-switching perspective, the language patterns and behaviors of linguistically diverse students started to be reframed from being "less knowledgeable about language" to being a "strategic, systematic language behavior" that draws upon the diverse linguistic resources of bilingual individuals. This early work built a foundation for researchers studying linguistically diverse students in educational settings (Cromdal & Aronsson, 2000; Jones & Thornborrow, 2004; Reyes, 2004).

As the field took a "translanguaging turn" (Garcia & Wei, 2014), researchers began to forgo discussions on code-switching in favor of the term *translanguaging*. Translanguaging refers to "new language practices that make visible the complexity of language" (Garcia & Wei, 2014, p. 3). Bilingual individuals, therefore, draw from diverse and multiple linguistic resources within a unitary linguistic system to challenge the idea that bilinguals are two monolinguals in one. With the increased interest in translanguaging, researchers and scholars have engaged in lively discussions on the differences between code-switching and translanguaging (e.g., MacSwan, 2017), understanding translanguaging as a theory of language (Cummins, 2017; Otheguy et al., 2019), and understanding translanguaging as a pedagogical endeavor (Probyn, 2019; Wu & Lin, 2019). These lively discussions have resulted in literature reviews (Canagarajah, 2011; Poza, 2017) and recent theoretical and conceptual debates on what the term translanguaging means in relation to adages like *additive bilingualism, code-switching, subtractive bilingualism*, and the like (Cummins, 2017; Otheguy et al., 2019; MacSwan, 2017).

Much of the debate on translanguaging and code-switching focuses on the nature of linguistic systems. Translanguaging scholars argue that translanguaging, as a theory of language, views bilingualism as a unified linguistic system, while contending that code-switching is based on bilinguals having two separate linguistic systems. This debate is not new. In 2000, Genesse published a chapter in *Bilingualism Reader* (Wei, 2000) titled "Early Bilingual Language Development: One Language or Two?" In that chapter, Genesse makes a strong argument as to why "young bilingual children are psycholinguistically able to differentiate two languages from the earliest stages of bilingual development and that they can use their two languages in functionally differentiated ways, thereby providing evidence of differentiated underlying language systems" (p. 327). The study of translanguaging shifted from arguments like Genesse's to viewing language as a unified system, rather a differentiated one.

In *Becoming Biliterate*, I wanted to step away from these sometimes inconclusive discussions of how bilingualism and biliteracy can be viewed as either "one language system" or "separate systems" (Genesee, 2000). My work with Emma suggested that becoming biliterate was more than learning the linguistic aspects of two named languages – Japanese and English – and how she transferred those linguistic aspects (e.g., language forms and grammatical structures) when reading and writing. In many ways, Emma did not see her participation in different linguistic communities as separate, but rather that her engagement with language and others permeated linguistic boundaries allowing her to live in "simultaneous worlds" (Gregory et al., 2004; Kenner, 2004).

For similar reasons, readers will not find much debate on the nature of language as unified or differentiated linguistic systems. I bring the premise to the work in this book that language is about, first and foremost, meaning construction – meaning constructed with text and meaning within one's life story. As such, I propose that translanguaging and code-switching are not competing concepts, if code-switching is redefined with contemporary, asset-oriented views of language.

It is within this context that revisiting my data with Emma became almost essential to better understand what it means to become biliterate from the perspective of the child. I wondered how the theoretical and conceptual frames of translanguaging could relate to not only my work with Emma but also my current study, *Revaluing Readers and Families*. I also wondered how to connect notions of translanguaging with the study of miscues and code-switching through the study of discourses, or language-in-use, and Discourses as an identity kit (Gee, 2002). Thus, revisiting studies have a history and that history has to be reexamined in light of the changing discourses and developing knowledge coming out of fields of study. The translanguaging turn is an illustrative example of how the evolving and shifting discourses in a field, one with a long history built on sociolinguistic perspectives of code-switching, can shift the conversation around the process of becoming biliterate.

Becoming Bilingual Readers as a Follow-Up to Becoming Biliterate

Becoming Biliterate focused on the complexity to which Emma became biliterate as she navigated four written language forms: Hiragana, Katakana, and Kanji in Japanese and the Roman alphabet in English, in reading and writing. Through the process of becoming biliterate, Emma actively defined her sense of self, gained access into the social and cultural spaces around her, and attended to her own social, cognitive, and emotional well-being.

In *Becoming Biliterate*, I wanted to help recapture a space for critical thought around languages and literacies. The very foundation of the book lied on notions that languages, both written and spoken, play substantive roles in learning and identity. Emma was born in Tokyo, Japan and from that time onward, she was socialized into ways of using Japanese and English at home. Although her father and I tried to divide language use at home (I spoke to Emma in English while Jay spoke in Japanese), language boundaries were permeable and often crossed. For instance, I read both English and Japanese books to Emma. Her favorite English book was *Elmer Blunt's Open House* (Novak, 1996), which I read repeatedly over the course of 2 years. At the same time, I also read Japanese storybooks that were mostly given to her by her grandparents. *おつきさまこんばんは [Good Evening, Moon]* (Hayashi, 1986) was a favorite of hers, and triggered her to start pointing to the moon and saying, "Konbawa," or good evening.

Emma's learning did not exist in isolation of outside social and cultural influences because, as researchers suggest, learning is inherently a sociocultural process. A sociocultural perspective on learning highlights how children's knowledge about written languages is the result of engaging in social activities with others. Emma wrote cards to her family and read the outside of cookie boxes, which often triggered a response from her father or me. This perspective encourages us to view learning through the navigation of home and community social structures so that children, like Emma, interact with different types of reading and writing practices in diverse languages (Taylor, 1983).

By participating in activities around language, for instance, Emma learned through English and Japanese and learned about them. Language became the medium through which relationships with family members developed and changed. As we actively engaged Emma in reading and writing activities, she could take on different roles and participate in social and cultural activities at home (Rogoff, 2003). Emma may have been a listener in one context, but in another, she attempted to recreate language for her own purposes based on what she already experienced.

Taking a sociocultural view of learning, I viewed Emma's biliteracy learning through the process of *becoming*, with a particular focus on Emma's early writing. In this process, becoming biliterate was more than learning the linguistic aspects of two named languages – Japanese and English – and how she transferred those linguistic aspects (e.g., language forms and grammatical structures) when reading and writing. That argument seemed secondary to how Emma made sense of and questioned herself over time.

By the time Emma was 5 years old, she was a novice bilingual reader and writer. Table 0.1 shows the range of writing and drawing artifacts that I collected between the ages of 3 and 7 years. These artifacts were categorized as self-produced, meaning that Emma created them herself on blank paper. The table is broken down into four main categories: writing in English, writing in Japanese, writing in both English and Japanese, and drawing only images. Artifacts that included both writing and drawing were counted toward the writing categories.

As Table 0.1 shows, Emma's use of English decreased from the ages of 3 and 5, while she wrote more in Japanese. Writing in English increased, however, when Emma entered kindergarten at 5 years old. By this time, Emma's English writing became more sophisticated. She wrote lists, explored with fonts by writing in bubble letters and cursive, and created storybooks. She was speaking English and Japanese inside and outside the home, as well as participating in a variety of social practices and developing relationships with

Table 0.1 Emma's Self-Produced Writing and Drawing Samples by Language Between 3 and 7 Years Old

Languages	*Age*							
	3–4 years old		*4–5 years old*		*5–6 years old*		*6–7 years old*	
English	76	56.7%	30	36.6%	37	58.7%	70	88.2%
Japanese	0	0	20	24.4%	20	31.7%	3	3.2%
Both	1	.7%	3	3.7%	3	4.8%	0	0
Image-only	55	41.0%	29	35.4%	3	4.8%	20	21.5%
Total	132		82		63		93	

other people in her environment. Then, one November evening before bed, Emma who was three months into kindergarten, said to her father, "Daddy, I don't want to be Japanese anymore."

Emma's comment was a passing but critical moment. Why would an early proficient bilingual/biliterate child who has a wealth of working knowledge about both Japanese and English suggest to her father that she wanted to change part of her cultural, language, and national identities? Answering this question was not easy; two months later Emma asked me, "If I was born in the Year of the Tiger, why do I speak English?" In addition, three months later, she wrote her name on her English homework in Japanese next to her English name. When I asked her why she did so, she replied, "Because I'm the only one in my class who can speak Japanese, so no one will know what I am writing."

Emma's comments suggest that language is much more than written and oral forms, words, and discourses. Language also embodies identities that connect people to their social groups; it can align speakers with particular groups, while creating an otherness for those outside the group (Wei, 2000). Being able to control and demonstrate proficiency in multiple written languages and spoken discourses is not sufficient to define what it means to become biliterate. It also means being able to understand the multiple social and cultural spaces within which one participates.

In trying to make sense of Emma's shifting identities, I found a breadth of data that pointed to the ideological struggles that undergird the process of becoming biliterate. These ideological struggles not only manifested themselves in how Emma talked about herself. They were also reflected in her writing. Table 0.1 shows that there was a drastic increase in writing in English between the ages of 6 and 7 years when Emma was in first grade. Unlike in the previous year, this increase is alongside a significant decrease in writing in Japanese at home.

Completing classwork and homework were expected tasks in kindergarten. While classwork was done regularly from the first day of school, Emma's teacher sent homework from January in order to give her kindergarten students time to adjust to in-school routines. Work done in class evolved around projects, center activities, and hands-on engagement in reading activities; participation in these activities did not always result in tangible products. Emma also completed commercial worksheets for handwriting practice, math, and isolated reading skills (such as practicing alphabetic letters and phonics). These worksheets were then sent home at the end of the week in Emma's communication folder.

Over Emma's kindergarten year, I collected 84 pieces of work that were sent home from school in Emma's communication folder. Commercial worksheets, both done in school and sent home for homework, consisted of 88% of the work and handwriting made up the largest category. After handwriting, worksheets that focused on alphabetic letters and letter–sound relationships were the next largest category, and this category was followed by the focus on individual words. If this amount of work is put into perspective to what she was producing at home during the same time frame, or at ages 5–6, Emma produced 63 writing (using both English and Japanese) and drawing artifacts at home. At ages of 4–5, Emma created 82 writing and drawing artifacts at home. Emma completed more worksheets during her kindergarten year (at least those that were sent home) than writing and drawing artifacts at home.

While kindergarten was framed by the idea of adjustment to school, first grade was characterized by the idea that students should be reading by the end of first grade. This tone was set before Emma left kindergarten. At Emma's kindergarten parent–teacher conferences in April, Emma's teacher stated that while students were not pushed to read by the end of kindergarten, they were expected to be reading by the end of their first-grade year. Emma's first-grade teacher emphasized literature, reading and writing in the classroom, and took an integrated approach to curriculum. When I asked Emma about her reflections of elementary school after entering middle school, she quickly commented that her first-grade teacher was her favorite (next to her fifth-grade teacher). The highlight of the year, which Emma has taken with her throughout her years of schooling, was the restaurant The Funky Monkey Café that Emma's teacher organized and to which all the parents were invited. The class read about animals and their habitats, went to the grocery store to buy food, and created menus, placemats, decorations, and other materials that they needed to convert their classroom into a restaurant. This type of integrated and wholistic approach to curriculum created an authentic engagement with reading, writing, and learning that heightened Emma's positive experiences in the classroom of her first-grade year.

While this may be the case, other trends that started in kindergarten continued. With the focus on having children read by the end of first grade, emphasis was placed on skills that were deemed necessary for or a part of reading. These skills were taught through worksheets that were done at school and as homework. In addition to the persistent use of commercial worksheets, the uses of English and Japanese not only in school but also at home continued to evolve. Underlying these shifts were ideological tensions around language and their ties to identity and access to school.

Similar to kindergarten, Emma completed classwork in the form of worksheets. The majority of first-grade worksheets, however, came out of workbooks created by publishing companies. The teacher tore out the pages that needed to be completed and the students did so as part of the classroom routine. These workbook pages, as well as photocopied worksheets, were also sent home for homework. Unlike kindergarten, Emma received homework by the end of September, and completed it anywhere from two to three times a week. Home reading also became an integral part of homework. Emma could read either by herself or with me, and I had to sign the home reading log to acknowledge that Emma read.

Emma's first-grade year saw a drastic increase in the amount of completed work (both school work and homework) sent home in her communication folder. I collected 562 pieces of work that were sent home over the course of first grade, and 94% of those 562 artifacts were worksheets or workbooks pages. I combined any type of math-related work under the general category of math, which consisted of 40% of Emma's completed work sent home. The other 60% focused on English Language Arts, more specifically on reading, writing, speaking, and listening.

The largest category of worksheets centered on individual words. Emma had to circle the word with a certain beginning letter sound or vowel sound or fill in sentences with words from the word families for that week. After the focus on words, Emma completed a number of worksheets that addressed reading comprehension. In addition to worksheets, Emma brought home some pieces that consisted of self-writing. For instance, Emma wrote sentences like, "The cat is fat" and "The pig is under the green sun" for word study instruction.

The types of reading and writing that Emma did at school was the antithesis of what she did at home. Emma's reading and writing at home were original; they were about Emma as a developing biliterate child. At school, reading and writing practices were about recreating an autonomous model of literacy that focuses on a skill-based view of reading and writing isolated from individuals as social and cultural beings (Street & Street, 1991). By reproducing autonomous literacy skills, Emma was acquiring membership into school and learning what school was all about. What school privileged and the texts that Emma produced as a result had little to do with the knowledge and identities that Emma actively constructed at home before entering kindergarten and first grade. School was primarily about acquiring membership into a community that had particular ways of doing, talking, acting, and thinking. In actuality, Emma's biliteracy was irrelevant to school; becoming biliterate was counterproductive to becoming a student.

In sum, becoming biliterate cannot be detached from the larger social, cultural, and ideological educational policies that support oral proficiency, reading, and writing in English (Auerbach, 1993; Halcon, 2001; Schieffelin et al., 1998; Woolard, 1998). Many of these ideologies around language and literacy were transmitted through day-to-day interactions with school work and homework. The sheer enormity and quantity of work that focused on the transmission of isolated skills affected the ways in which Emma used languages. In the act of doing, Emma developed identities that aligned herself with group membership into school; she learned how to write, act, talk, and read like a student.

As a follow-up to *Becoming Biliterate*, *Becoming Bilingual Readers* draws on sociocultural concepts of identities, ideologies, and social practices involving reading and writing to explore how becoming a reader provides a way to examine how biliteracy is constitutive of one's developing identity and agency within and across home and school contexts. Researchers (e.g., Gee,

2002; Packer & Goicoechea, 2000) describe how identities are constructed within social spaces, which then leads to the argument of how the process of becoming involves three interconnected domains: the person, the place (or context), and the things (or objects and tools) that are part of social activities. It is, however, not just the interactions across these domains that result in learning to become biliterate.

The process of becoming also refers to how these domains transform and change over time – a concept that *Becoming Biliterate* did not tackle. While we may consider becoming through social and personal transformation, this transformation does not happen outside of any social context or the tools within social activities. When Emma learned to write her name in three Japanese scripts and in the Roman alphabet, she not only transformed the details of the script to make them more in line with conventional Japanese forms but she also wrote on cards she sent to her grandparents who lived in Japan. Within each activity, she transformed the relationships she had with people, the context within which those individuals participated, and the writing system themselves, which can only be examined through a temporal perspective to learning.

The idea that a Japanese- and English-speaking child, like Emma, has what it means to be biliterate in first grade can look very different from what it means in fifth grade and will look very different again when in college. The move from first grade to fifth grade to college occurs on a longer timescale composed of shorter ones, such as writing a note to your friend in Japanese, reading your English book as part of a school assignment, and drawing a picture of your family living across transnational boundaries in Japan. Each of these acts, or literacy events (Barton & Hamilton, 1998), provides a snapshot of how a child can "be biliterate" or how they present themselves to other people, but it does not necessarily get to the process of becoming biliterate.

Becoming biliterate, rather, involves changes and transformation over time. In other words, how does bilingual children's language use change over short- and long-term timescales? How are bilingual children recognized by others at any given moment in time? How do they select and transform the tools available to them in their practices? How do they redefine what it means "to be" biliterate from activity to activity over longer timescales? While we can examine the events and the resulting artifacts, understanding the process of becoming requires looking at what it means "to be" over longer timescales (Compton-Lilly, 2017).

To "be biliterate" can be thought of as an identity label. This label is constructed in activities that result from the process of becoming biliterate, which is one of struggle and contestation. As the tools and contexts evolve, so does the process of becoming biliterate, as each is constitutive of the other. In this sense, the identification of "being biliterate" does not capture the process and should not be seen with preconceived notions of what it means to become biliterate. Rather, I contend that each individual constructs their own understandings of what it means to be biliterate through the ongoing and never-ending process of becoming biliterate.

This volume will pick up from *Becoming Biliterate* to address the area of bilingual reading to consider the process of becoming a bilingual reader through the documentation, observation, reflection, and collaboration captured in Biographic Biliteracy Profiles (henceforth called the Profiles). Analyzing and organizing the data into Profiles mean developing an asset-oriented narrative about children's biliteracy configurations through humanistic and advocacy perspectives to assessment. Through this perspective, children are seen as holding a variety of positionalities across social and participatory contexts. They are members of families, students in school, and members of church communities, for instance. These positionalities also lead to the existence of different and sometimes competing goals. An advocacy perspective suggests that one goal is not privileged over others, and the individual – teacher, researcher, and specialist – attempts to capture the complexity of the activities at hand.

Through the Profiles, I will not only revisit Emma's biliteracy through the lens of her becoming a bilingual reader but also introduce the children from three bilingual families, Thomas, Jenny, Sophie, and Mai, to illustrate how bilingual reading behaviors connect to linguistic action and identity enactments and are mediated by other people and things. To introduce the complexity of bilingual reading behaviors in relation to becoming a bilingual reader, I will engage in what Taylor (in Kabuto, 2017) describes as archeological reconstructions of children's individual literacy knowledge through the Profiles. The Profiles capture "the complexity of the richness and diversity of children's literacy experiences" (Taylor in Kabuto, 2017, p. 110). They are constructed through observations (what children do) and interviews (what children say) about themselves as readers and their reading.

At the same time, the Profiles are narratives that involve how I, or anyone who writes them, engage in a certain type of recognition work as I acknowledge the work in which linguistically diverse children engage to interpret print in different named languages to create patterns of behaviors. I have the responsibility to view linguistically diverse children through a humanistic perspective. This perspective refers to how children are viewed as social actors with a personal history and living in a family and community context whose reading behaviors are like fingerprints – unique and individual to each child.

Rather than present the Profiles of each of the children individually, I draw and present themes from the Profiles to better understand how notions of translanguaging, bilingual reading behaviors, and identity intersect and inform our understanding of what it means to become biliterate.

Each chapter will present a theme threaded through the Profiles. Chapters 1 and 2 will provide a foundation for using the Profiles as an assessment tool that builds on reflection and collaboration to make learning public (Pierce & Ordoñez-Jasis, 2018). Chapter 3 addresses bilingual reading behaviors as a unified process of meaning construction through the presentation of Sophie's and Mai's Profiles. Chapter 4 focuses on two novice bilingual readers, Jenny and Emma, to discuss how code-switching provides as a means to slow down the conversational moves to determine how a translanguaging context is co-constructed through in-the-moment assessment and changes over time. Chapter 5 links bilingual reading abilities and identities through Sophie's and Jenny's Profiles to consider their identity maps.

The goal of this volume is to address questions related to (a) what a bilingual reader's self-identity means in becoming biliterate, (b) the differences between code-switching and translanguaging, and (c) how these linguistic behaviors change and shift across people, things, space, and timescales. By presenting the Profiles, this book will include practical applications of observing and documenting bilingual readers.

References

Auer, P. (Ed.). (1999). *Code-switching in conversation.* Routledge.

Auerbach, E. R. (1993). Reexamining English only in ESL classrooms. *TESOL Quarterly, 27*(1), 9–32.

Barton, D., & Hamilton, M. (1998). *Local literacies: Reading and writing in one community.* Routledge.

Blommaert, J., & Verschueren, J. (1998). The role of language in European nationalist ideologies. In B. Schieffelin, K. Woolard, & P. Kroskrity (Eds.), *Language ideologies: Practice and theory.* Oxford University Press.

Canagarajah, S. (2011). Translanguaging in the classroom: Emerging issues for research and pedagogy. *Applied Linguistics Review, 2,* 1–28.

Compton-Lilly, C. (2017). *Reading students' lives: Literacy learning across time.* Routledge.

Cromdal, J., & Aronsson, K. (2000). Footing in bilingual play. *Journal of Sociolinguistics, 4*(3), 435–457.

Cummins, J. (2017). Teaching minoritized students: Are additive approaches legitimate? *Harvard Educational Review, 87*(3), 404–425.

Garcia, O. (2009). *Bilingual education in the 21st century: A global perspective.* Wiley-Blackwell.

Garcia, O., & Wei, L. (2014). *Translanguaging: Language, bilingualism, and education.* Palgrave MacMillan.

Gee, J. (2002). A sociocultural perspective on early literacy development. In S. Neuman & D. Dickinson (Eds.), *Handbook of early literacy research* (pp. 30–42). Guilford Press.

Genesee, F. (2000). Early bilingual language development: One language or two. In L. Wei (Ed.), *The bilingualism reader* (pp. 327–343). Routledge.

Gort, M. (2006). Strategic codeswitching, interliteracy, and other phenomena of emergent bilingual writing: Lessons from a first grade dual language classrooms. *Journal of Early Childhood Literacy, 6*(3), 323–354.

Gregory, E., Long, S., & Volk, D. (2004). A sociocultural approach to learning. In E. Gregory, S. Long, & D. Volk (Eds.), *Many pathways to literacy: Young children learning with siblings, grandparents, peers and communities* (pp. 6–20). Routledge-Falmer.

Gumperz, J. (1982). *Discourse strategies.* Cambridge University Press.

Halcon, J. (2001). Mainstream ideology and literacy instruction for Spanish-speaking children. In M. d. l. L. Reyes & J. Halcon (Eds.), *The best for our children: Critical perspectives on literacy for Latino students*. Teachers College Press.

Hayashi, A. (1986). *Otsukisama konbawa*. Fukuinkan Shoten.

Heller, M. (1988). Strategic ambiguity: Codeswitching in the management of conflict. In M. Heller (Ed.), *Codeswitching: Anthropological and sociolinguistic perspectives* (pp. 77–96). Mouton de Gruyter.

Jones, R., & Thornborrow, J. (2004). Floors, talk and the organization of classroom activities. *Language in Society*, *33*(3), 399–423.

Kabuto, B. (2010). *Becoming biliterate: Identity, ideology, and learning to read and write in two languages*. Routledge.

Kabuto, B. (Ed.). (2017). *Teaching without testing: Assessing the complexity of children's literacy learning* (D. Taylor, Ed.). Garn Press Women Scholars Series Volume 2. Garn Press.

Kabuto, B., & Martens, P. (Eds.). (2014). *Linking families, learning, and schooling: Parent-researcher perspectives*. Routledge.

Kenner, C. (2004). Living in simultaneous worlds: Difference and integration in bilingual script- learning. *Bilingual Education and Bilingualism*, 7(1), 43–61.

MacSwan, J. (2017). A multilingual perspective on translanguaging. *American Educational Research Journal*, *54*(1), 167–201.

Novak, M. (1996). *Elmer Blunt's open house*. Scholastic.

Otheguy, R., García, O., & Reid, W. (2019). A translanguaging view of the linguistic system of bilinguals. *Applied Linguistics Review*, *10*(4), 625–651.

Packer, M. J., & Goicoechea, J. (2000). Sociocultural and constructivist theories of learning: Ontology, not just epistemology. *Educational psychologist*, *35*(4), 227–241.

Pierce, K. M., & Ordoñez-Jasis, R. (2018). *Going public with assessment: A community practice approach*. National Council of Teachers of English.

Poza, L. (2017). Translanguaging: Definitions, implications, and further needs in burgeoning inquiry. *Berkeley Review of Education*, *6*(2), 101–128.

Probyn, M. (2019). Pedagogical translanguaging and the construction of science knowledge in a multilingual South African classroom: Challenging monoglossic/post-colonial orthodoxies. *Classroom Discourse*, *10*(3–4), 216–236.

Reyes, I. (2004). Functions of code switching in schoolchildren's conversations. *Bilingual Research Journal*, *28*(1), 77–98.

Rogoff, B. (2003). *The cultural nature of human development*. Oxford University Press.

Schieffelin, B., Woolard, K., & Paul, K. (Eds.). (1998). *Language ideologies: Practice and theory*. Oxford University Press.

Sefton-Green, J., & Rowsell, J. (Eds.). (2015). *Learning and literacy over time: Longitudinal perspectives*. Routledge.

Street, J. C., & Street, B. V. (1991). The schooling of literacy. In D. Barton & R. Ivanic (Eds.), *Writing in the community* (Vol. 6, pp. 143–166). Sage.

Taylor, D. (1983). *Family literacy: Young children learning to read and write*. Heinemann.

Wei, L. (1999). The 'why' and 'how' questions in the analysis of conversational code-switching. In P. Auer (Ed.), *Code-switching in conversation* (pp. 156–176). Routledge.

Wei, L. (Ed.). (2000). *The bilingualism reader*. Routledge.

Woolard, K. (1998). Language ideology as a field of inquiry. In B. Schieffelin, K. Woolard, & K. Paul (Eds.), *Language ideologies: Practice and theory*. Oxford University Press.

Wu, Y., & Lin, A. M. (2019). Translanguaging and trans-semiotising in a CLIL biology class in Hong Kong: Whole-body sense-making in the flow of knowledge co-making. *Classroom Discourse*, *10*(3–4), 252–273.

1 Culturally Relevant Assessment Practices for Linguistically Diverse Readers

In the field of education, the term *assessment* does not always have the gentlest connotation. Most people will immediately associate it with high-stakes state testing, commercial standardized assessments, teacher accountability, grade-level standards, and yearly progress reports, all of which index some sort of constructed notion of success or failure. Regardless of research showing that standardized assessments are limited in capturing the breadth and richness of knowledge (National Research Council, 2001), they have in fact become a big business with for-profit corporations and publishers controlling the narrative around who is learning and who is not (Cody, 2014; Pierce & Ordoñez-Jasis, 2018). Creating a singular view of what and how students should learn in school and how educational institutions should assess that learning, the term can lead ultimately to dread and stress, especially for historically marginalized students of color (Willis, 2019).

Among the marginalized groups who have not always been treated well by educational assessment practices are linguistically diverse students. In this book, I will use the term *linguistically diverse* to discuss the general language diversity of and across groups of people. To talk more specifically about the individual readers in this book, I will use some form of the terms *bilingualism* and *biliteracy* because all the readers herein speak, read, and write in two named languages (i.e., Spanish, Greek, Japanese, and English).

Educational assessment practices of linguistically diverse students have historically been built on an ideology that privileges English over home or heritage languages (Sanchez et al., 2013). In K-12 settings, the pedagogical norm that still dominates today is one of language separation existing in models ranging from an English-only curriculum to organizing languages throughout the day by context (like home, school, or subject), by participants (like the English teacher or the Spanish teacher), and by materials (the English book or the Japanese book). Language separation purposely limits the ways that languages can be used in fluid and natural ways and perpetuates the belief among many in and out of education that the observable range of diverse language behaviors exhibited by bilingual and biliterate students are problems rather than resources (Macías, 2016). The argument goes something like this: languages need to be kept separate and differentiated, and

DOI: 10.4324/9781003045984-2

language mixing is an indicator of confusion or a lack of knowledge. In other words, how else were linguistically diverse students expected to learn English if they were allowed to use their other language in learning and assessment? This line of thought insists that using English as the medium for instruction not only helps students learn English faster but it is also a tool for assimilation into US schooling and society.

Over time, depending on English to assess linguistically diverse students has devalued the range of diverse linguistic behaviors and practices within families and communities, thereby creating a disconnect between home and school. In their research with culturally and linguistically diverse families, Manyak and Dantas (2010) argued, "A number of research studies focused on families and schooling have demonstrated that educators may find themselves confused by families whose values and practices differ greatly from their own, and, at times, develop negative views about such families' interest and support of their children's schooling" (p. 3). Manyak and Dantas illustrated how teachers thought they should lower their academic expectations of linguistically diverse children in their classrooms because they felt that these children did not have quality, stimulating experiences or spoke another language at home.

Families are not immune to the disconnect and can engage in family language planning, defined as "a deliberate attempt at practicing a particular language use pattern and particular literacy practices within home domains and among family members" (Curdt-Christiansen, 2009, p. 352) that can support (or not support) linguistic diversity. When families see the value in linguistic diversity, they are more likely to provide resources and environments that will support their aspirations for their children (Curdt-Christiansen & La Morgia, 2018). Conversely, families who feel that their home languages have negative impacts on their children's academic progress change how they support their children's uses of their home languages (Curdt-Christiansen & La Morgia, 2018; Ren & Hu, 2013).

Of educational importance is how assessment practices that privilege and depend on the use of English create not just a deficit-oriented lens, ignoring the ways in which knowledge manifests itself in the breadth of literacy practices and events in which linguistically diverse students participate. The dependence on English has also produced a racially biased approach to assessment. Standardized tests contain cultural biases resulting in poor performance by linguistically diverse students (Artiles et al., 2002; Everett et al., 2013). For instance, New York State's yearly English Language Arts exams are given to students in grades 3–6. Based on the 2019 NYS ELA exam results (https://data.nysed.gov/assessment38.php?subject=ELA&year=2019&state=yes), when results are disaggregated by ethnicity, 36% of Hispanic or Latino students were deemed proficient compared to 51% of White students and 67% of Asian or Pacific Islander students. These categories come directly from NYS ELA data reports. What is striking is that only 9% of English Language Learners were deemed proficient compared to non-English Language

Learners. Students in other socially disadvantaged categories – economically disadvantaged, students in foster care, migrant populations, and the homeless – performed far worse than students in nonsocially disadvantaged categories. It is this type of data, in fact, that has led to students of color and linguistically diverse students being overly identified to special education and other remedial services and has created a narrative that blames and associates race with academic performance (Everett et al., 2013).

Standardized and high-stakes testing tells us less about what students have actually learned and more about the social inequities that exist in society. As a racially biased practice, standardized assessments reproduce "a prejudice against someone based on race, when those prejudices are reinforced by systems or power" (Oluo, 2019, p. 26). The dominance of standardized testing reproduces systemic inequalities that have serious implications for teacher ratings, funding, and school resources. Schools with particular populations of students who are deemed as underperforming may receive different types of curricular structures and are more closely monitored by the state than schools who are performing up to state expectations.

Similarly, the process of state testing is prejudicial against groups of students. Latinx and Black students are shown to consistently underperform when compared to White and Asian students. The overperforming of Asian and Pacific Islanders groups a broad range of the world's population into a singular stereotype placing undue burdens and expectations on these individuals (Olou, p. 191). This "model minority myth" diminishes the variety of bias and racist practices they encounter both in and out of schools (Kim, 2020). While we have known, for many years, that standardized assessment practices reflect the social inequalities in society, educational systems do more of the same rather than break the cycle of educational inequality. This point has raised a call for alternative forms of culturally relevant assessment practices (Ascenzi-Moreno, 2018; Everett et al., 2013; Rueda & Windmueller, 2006).

Biographic Biliteracy Profiles as a Culturally Relevant Assessment Practice

Set against the backdrop of developing more culturally relevant and linguistically inclusive ways to assess diverse students, the Profiles are a means of providing an alternative perspective to the deficit-oriented lens about race and language perpetuated by standardized and commercial assessments. Culturally relevant assessments are based on the "cultural knowledge, prior experiences, frames of reference, and performance styles of ethnically diverse students to make learning more relevant to and effective [for students]" (Gay, 2000, p. 29). They are tools for not just evaluating students but also positioning them as knowledgeable socially, culturally, and linguistically capable beings, as they draw from their range of linguistic knowledge and language resources to communicate what they know. A culturally relevant assessment process for reading, however, is more than documenting readers transacting with text. While standardized assessment practices are more about measuring one student relative to another, culturally relevant assessment practices document cultural knowledge, prior experiences, and performance styles of bilingual students to understand how and what students know. These assessment practices draw from a collaborative process that engages students, teachers, families, and other stakeholders.

The Profiles are built from multiple data sources that include, but are not limited to, observations, interviews, reading records, work samples, and accompanying dialogue. The aim of the Profiles is to capture student diversity and the linguistic flexibility that is needed as readers transact with texts and develop biliterate identities. As Pierce and Ordoñez-Jasis (2018) found, while teachers work with a variety of data sources every day in their day-to-day interactions with students, in documenting what students know and providing them feedback to create an assessment loop, they do not always value this type of formative assessment process.

The Profiles are designed to place the student and language back into the center of the assessment process so that it is a collaborative, reflective, and inquiry-based process. As I will explain in the next section, the Profiles originated from a larger study, *Revaluing Readers and Families*, that engaged family members in reading practices and events in strategic ways to build an environment around reading as a reflective process so that parents learn about not only their children as readers but also the reading process.

Focusing on collective expertise, it took parents and their children working together, reflecting on miscues, responding to text, and asking questions to create a shared goal of supporting their children as readers. As we did, we engaged in *in-the-moment assessment*, which refers to spontaneous evaluation and feedback provided to bilingual readers in order to move them forward in their thinking. The in-the-moment assessment requires considering and strategically responding to information to scaffold learners.

As Vanlommel and Schildkamp (2019) describe, data can have different meanings to different people. The types of data we collect and the information to which we respond reflect beliefs about teaching and learning (Harmey, 2021; Pierce & Ordoñez-Jasis, 2018; Vanlommel & Schildkamp, 2019). As such, we have the power to shift beliefs and perspectives, and this point is critical to advocate for linguistic diversity by placing assessment in a translanguaging space. It is for this reason that this book is not a how-to book but rather one that provides theoretical dialogues to challenge unexamined assumptions about bilingual reading behaviors, bilingual readers, and linguistically diverse families and how we know what these readers know.

As a culturally relevant assessment tool, the Profiles invite different perspectives and deprivatize the practice of assessment so that new ways of knowing are captured and actualized in the assessment process (Pierce & Ordoñez-Jasis, 2018). Encouraging new voices in the assessment process, particularly for linguistically diverse students, provides insights into the sense-making ways that draw on historical, social, and cultural knowledge. The use of culturally relevant assessment tools like the Profiles is a necessary step in advocating for antiracist assessment practices by situating learning experiences, literacy manifestations, and reading behaviors within an asset-oriented narrative.

Constructing Biographic Biliteracy Profiles

Biographic Biliteracy Profiles provide a common template for discussing the biliteracy configurations of the children and their families through a culturally responsive assessment lens. While Taylor (in Kabuto, 2017) used Biographic Literacy Profiles for exploring classroom activities and observations, the Profiles used herein contain data collected outside the classroom and in the context of the home and family. I draw on a combination of data that includes revisiting data from my study of Emma's process of becoming biliterate and *Revaluing Readers and Families.*

Emma participated in a variety of social practices that invoked both languages inside and outside of the home. Children play with friends; they may go to preschool or gym classes. Each of these practices has particular ways of using both oral and written language. Our move to New York from Japan when Emma was 2 years old heralded a switch in culture, social activities, and language use. Naturally, the Japanese-dominant community was replaced by an English-speaking environment. Yet, her father Jay and I tried to keep our language use consistent with the bilingual atmosphere that we created in Japan at home. Developing a linguistically diverse atmosphere allowed Emma to learn multiple written languages by becoming an active member of her home and community. Consequently, the nature of the social practices in which Emma participated was fluid and evolving as she grew older and her interests changed. Some of the major social practices that were influential in her everyday life include:

- Mommy and Me classes. Emma and I attended Mommy and Me classes two days a week. One class was for Japanese families and was run by a woman in our neighborhood. The other class was a gym class from a corporate, chain gym company.
- Play dates. Emma had regular play dates with both Japanese- and English-speaking children. I became friends with other Japanese wives who had also moved from Japan to New York, and our children became friends. We set up regular and rotating play dates for our children. Additionally, Emma had play dates with English-speaking friends from her Mommy and Me classes and her preschool classes.
- Birthday Parties. Birthday parties were a commonly occurring social event for Emma. She attended a variety of types of parties that included gym parties, dress-up parties, and cooking parties.

- Holidays. Holidays such as Halloween, Christmas, and Easter influenced the types of activities in which Emma participated within a calendar year. For example, when she went to see Santa, she wanted to write a letter, or when it was time for Halloween, she drew Halloween pictures and taped them on her bedroom door.
- Preschool. Emma attended a local preschool three hours a day starting at age 3. Emma's class was an English-dominant class; however, she had one Japanese-speaking friend named Keisuke in her 3-year-old class, who she knew before she entered preschool. On the other hand, her 4-year-old class consisted of all English-dominant children.
- Japanese school. Emma attended a weekly Japanese school at age 3 at the same time that she entered a 2-hour preschool class. She attended the preschool class for one year and then progressed to a Japanese kindergarten class. Japanese kindergarten starts from age 4 and lasts for 2 years; thus, Emma continued in kindergarten until age 6.
- Familial practices at home. This category covers a wide and general range of regular activities at home and consisted of activities performed using both languages. Emma watched English and Japanese videos, read books written in both languages, and played English and Japanese games. Emma also enjoyed completing Japanese activities books called *Shimajiro* with her father. This category also includes American popular culture activities for children, such as playing Barbies and collecting Disney Princesses.

The social practices that shaped Emma's experiences were rich, varied, and dynamic in their language and literacy uses, and were – importantly – highly complex. Although I have tried to categorize them here as separate entities for discussion's sake, the boundaries between these practices were fluid. Activities at home were influenced by holidays and play dates and her language use may have been tied not only to social practices but also to who the participants were in the immediate context. For instance, she often spoke with her friend Keisuke in Japanese in her English-speaking preschool because his language preference was Japanese. Therefore, in building relationships Emma did not necessarily see language learning as language separation, in which she needed to separate languages depending on context. Instead, Emma appeared to draw on a variety of linguistic resources to communicate with others and in the process constructed a translanguaging context.

My study of Emma's biliteracy suggested that becoming biliterate is a journey, and journeys take time. Because Emma was born into a biliterate home she encountered things around her in English and Japanese, and used language to build relationships, enter into relationships, and make sense of the ways in which languages organized her life. Life for Emma was made up of an endless amount of possibilities. Language provided a means to document the everyday happenings of the world around her. Over time, Emma's use of Japanese and English defined her self-in-practice – the active recreation of identity though the designing of texts. When Emma wrote in two languages, she reinforced her identity as a biliterate child.

Conversely, participation in school required Emma to redefine how English created a certain type of social and linguistic currency. While Emma spoke, read, and wrote in English from a young age, the substance of English she encountered in school was different than what she had previously experienced. In many ways, it did not match the fluid and dynamic uses of linguistic resources when reading and writing in English and Japanese which Emma experienced at home. The result was that she began to see an otherness in her identity.

This sense-of-otherness manifested itself in the ways that Emma talked about how English and Japanese allowed her access into not only school but also American society (Kristeva, 2003). Gee (2004) described the ways in which an individual can "despise" oneself, which will lead to "dynamics where there is more than one person in us." Gee (2004) stated, "We are multiple people. We have different identities, and those identities don't have to be compatible with each other. They can be at war with each other." As Emma ventured out into the world she did not always feel herself belonging to particular social groups or structures. When Emma said that she did not want to be Japanese anymore, it was not because she did not have access into English-speaking social structures or felt that Japanese was irrelevant in her life. In fact, two months later Emma began writing her name in Japanese next to the English representation of her name.

These observations, along with many more, led me to argue that language is a tool to develop spaces of possibility in an ever-changing world. Emma could be the unique person she was (and is) and could accommodate the ways in which life forced her to be multiple people. Reading and writing in a translanguaging context liberated Emma from the constraints of ideological beliefs that monolingualism is tied to social and linguistic competence.

Revaluing Readers and Families

Applying major themes that arose out of my study of Emma's biliteracy, *Revaluing Readers and Families* is premised on three key ideas that concluded *Becoming Biliterate*. First, readers need to develop healthy and positive identities. Readers come to school with tools from homes and families and these tools can be transformative agents in readers' understandings of what they see as they enter into new spaces and endure life's changes over time.

With mandated educational policies, readers may be constrained by scripted texts without allowing the language flexibility needed to take on new roles and voices. There is little to no attention to the social inequalities that children face, the economic disparities of schools that are labeled at-risk, and the identities and family histories that readers bring with them in the classroom. Rather, mandated polices justify "inert ideas" (Whitehead, 1925) or recreate the "banking system" (Freire, 2003) of education.

The second premise is that readers should be able to freely choose their mode of learning and expression. At home, Emma was able to freely choose her mode of learning from a range of linguistic possibilities and demonstrated behaviors that looked qualitatively different from monolingual children. As such, difference does not equate with difficulty.

Finally, *Revaluing Readers and Families* builds on the idea that readers are encouraged to become aware of their own thinking. This premise is captured by the concept of revaluing, which recognizes and legitimatizes the knowledge, thinking, and conscious expression of ideas so that readers are encouraged to use multiple languages in a variety of reading contexts. Readers are provided a space to became critical thinkers who engage in and try to problem-solve with language and texts through a transactive process.

To expand the study beyond *Becoming Biliterate*, *Revaluing Readers and Families* includes families to focus on how parents and their children defined and understood the children as readers through school-based labels such as *at-, above-, or below-grade level readers, English Language Learners,* or *bilingual students*. In this study, I explored how the term *reading ability* is an identity marker that is socially constructed by social, cultural, and temporal factors within families and school contexts. Common institutionalized discourses around special education and "grade-level" reading can have deficit orientations that reconstruct notions of what it means to "be a reader" within family and school contexts. Families do not necessarily interpret what it means to be a reader through single, decontextualized activities. Rather, they interpret and reinterpret the act of reading over time through transgenerational literacy practices. A transgenerational perspective on literacy practices forefronts the complexity of knowledge over time and space to integrate past histories, present experiences, and future possibilities. Within transgenerational literacy practices, reciprocal socialization among family members results in the sharing of knowledge about reading.

It is through that study that I met three bilingual families and studied how the families constructed narratives of their families' biliteracy as they made sense of their children's bilingual reading behaviors. Bilingual families provide a cautionary tale that labels like *English Language Learner, English as a New Language*, and even *bilingual* can privilege a one-size-fits-all perspective of linguistically diverse families and students that does not necessarily reflect their lived language experiences. While families and students may be considered "bilingual," each construct different types of identities and what it means to "be" and "become" bilingual and biliterate.

Thomas and Jenny

I first met Thomas and Jenny when Thomas was 12 years old and in the sixth grade, and Jenny was 5 years old and not yet in school. I will call this time period Phase I of the study. I revisited the family three years after Phase I when Thomas was 15 years old and in high school, and Jenny was

8 years old and in second grade. I will call this revisiting period Phase II. During Phase I of the study, Thomas attended a Spanish and English dual-language school in a large urban public school system. He had attended the school since kindergarten and was part of the first class to graduate from the school's dual-language program. The program consisted of an alternating language model in which language arts, mathematics, and science and social studies were taught in Spanish and English on alternating days, and students were expected to use them accordingly. Thomas considered himself a confident reader who enjoyed reading both English and Spanish texts, although he reported that it was difficult to find Spanish texts to read outside of school.

During Phase I of the study, Jenny was Spanish-dominant in speaking and listening, although she demonstrated some proficiency in understanding and speaking English. She demonstrated many effective beginning reading behaviors (Goodman et al., 2007). She enjoyed having books read to her, and she would construct stories based on the pictures in books. During this phase, Jenny was in the process of kindergarten screening, and Thomas and Jenny's mother Maria wanted Jenny to attend the same dual-language school as Thomas. After the screening, Maria excitedly reported that the teachers who screened Jenny were impressed that she could say her ABCs and count almost to 100.

When I met Jenny and Thomas in Phase II, Jenny was a second grader in the same dual-language school that Thomas had attended, and Thomas was in high school. While Maria was happy with Jenny's schooling experiences, she was not as happy with Thomas's high school experiences. Maria expressed disappointment in the fact that Thomas had rich language experiences while in the dual-language school, only to go to an English-dominant middle and high school.

Thomas's parents emigrated from Ecuador and met and married in the United States. Maria was Spanish-dominant in speaking, listening, reading, and writing. She had not finished high school, but this did not deter her from engaging in diverse reading experiences at home. She described reading to both her children from the time they were toddlers and read the Bible with her children on a daily basis. Maria used public resources to support language learning in the family. She took English language classes until she gave birth to Jenny.

Few books were present in Thomas's home, so Maria took Thomas and Jenny regularly to the library near the dual-language school because of its selection of text materials written in English and Spanish. When it was time for Thomas to start school, Maria sought a dual-language school. She traveled with Thomas for an hour each way for him to attend the school. Having her children attend a dual-language school was important to her. First, they lived in an area with high crime rate and low-income housing. She moved there because the price of renting an apartment was affordable. Maria felt that the downside was that she did not feel that the local school was suitable for her children because it was not a highly rated school. Second, Maria felt that she could be more involved in her children's education if they attended a dual-language school. In fact, she often talked about her experiences serving as a class mother for Thomas during Phase I. During Phase II, however, Maria decided to find employment near the dual-language school. She said that she was still close to Jenny's school, which allowed her to attend class trips, conferences, or other school activities.

Sophie

At the time of the study, Sophie was a 9-year-old fourth-grade student at a private, dual-language (Greek and English) school in a large urban city. She had attended the school since kindergarten. The dual-language model in Sophie's school focused on English to teach content (math, science, and social studies) and English Language Arts. Students received Greek language, reading, and writing instructions daily for one 45-minute period. This model was designed to serve the larger school population. The school was located in a predominantly Greek community in which families who attended the school had at least one parent who was a first-generation native Greek-speaker.

From the beginning of the study, Sophie articulated that she was more comfortable speaking, reading, and writing in English, although she said that she was able to communicate in Greek. Sophie lived a transnational lifestyle spending her summers in Greece with her aunts and grandmother. She said that she therefore felt more proficient in listening and speaking rather than reading and writing Greek.

Sophie's mother Frances is a native Greek speaker who is also fluent in English, while her father Steve is a monolingual English speaker. Sophie's parents provided a financially secure home environment. Frances held a corporate job for a major bank, and Steve worked for a manufacturing company. Sophie's parents reported that their main reason for sending Sophie to the dual-language school was to provide her with an education that included her Greek heritage. The school was in fact a major part of the Greek community and participated in several community Greek events throughout the year. While Sophie's parents felt that learning to read and write in Greek was important, they liked that the structure of the dual-language focused on English for teaching content. Both parents were more concerned about Sophie's grades in the content areas and English Language Arts than her performance in daily Greek instruction.

Mai

Mai was 8 years old and in second grade when her family participated in the study. Unlike the other children in the study, Mai was born in Japan and had lived there until her father's company moved them to the United

States when she was in kindergarten. Mai's family spent two years in California where she attended kindergarten and first grade, and then moved to New York. In New York, Mai attended an English-only public school in a middle-class suburban area and received English as Second Language classes three times a week. On Saturdays, Mai went to a Japanese school held in the local middle school. There, Mai took classes in Japanese language, reading, writing, Japanese history, and mathematics. Japanese heritage was an integral part of the curriculum, which followed one that you would find in Japan. Books and other curricular materials for the Japanese school were supplied by the Japanese ministry.

Mai did not always demonstrate confidence in her speaking, reading, and writing in English. When encouraged to use Japanese, however, she enjoyed participating in conversations and reading and writing activities. Her parents, Mariko and Taki, were native Japanese-speaking individuals, and Taki was more comfortable speaking in English than Mariko. Both of Mai's parents were educated and had graduated from college in Japan. While Taki worked for a global corporation, Mariko left her job as a flight attendant after she married Taki. Mariko expressed that she could not help Mai at home and worried about her progress in second grade. In particular, Mai was often recommended for different types of academic interventions and social support groups in the public school. While Mai was outgoing and developed friendships at Japanese school, she was quiet at her public school. Because Mai's family was expected to return to Japan within three years of arriving in New York, Mariko was not overly concerned with Mai becoming proficient in English while living in the United States.

Profile Data

A research assistant and I met with two of the three families above over a 10-week period, with each weekly session ranging from 1 to 1.5 hours. Livia was my assistant when I worked with Thomas and Jenny, while Despina worked with Sophie and me. During this time, I collected a range of data for the Profiles.

The sessions began with informal interviews during which parents responded to questions regarding their children's progress in school, how they saw the school's role in providing services to support their children's reading and writing, and their goals for their children's literacy progress. I interviewed the children to inquire into their hobbies and recreational activities, how they felt about school, their friends and family, and how they felt about reading at home and at school. Subsequent sessions also included informal interviews about how school was progressing, which served an important purpose in "catching up" with the families from previous sessions. In addition to the informal conversations, I interviewed the parents and children using the Burke Reading Inventory (Goodman et al., 2005), which is composed of questions designed to target readers' beliefs about reading and their perceptions of the reading process.

I conducted observations and collected data and documentation of reading activities. These activities were composed of oral reading and retelling data regarding both parents and children. The children were encouraged to select their own books, especially books written in their other language. The parents also read books or magazines that either they selected or I suggested. They were encouraged to select materials in the language in which they were most comfortable reading. While for some parents, the language may have been English, others selected books written in Spanish or Japanese. Table 1.1 provides a list and description of the books that Emma, Mai, Thomas, Jenny, and Sophie read in the sessions that are part of the Profiles included in this book.

Finally, I used Family Retrospective Miscue Analysis (Family RMA) with the families in sessions that followed the oral readings and retellings (see Appendix A and Kabuto, 2009 for a more detailed discussion on Family

Table 1.1 Texts Read as Part of the Profiles

Title and Author	*Story Synopsis*	*Special Features*
あひるのたまご *[Ahiru no Tamago]* (Sato, 1995)	This picture book tells the story of a grandmother who helps to hatch a duck's eggs. The characters are various farm animals who interact with the grandmother.	The picture book has strong picture support. It is written in Japanese Hiragana.
Alexander and the Wind-Up Mouse (Lionni, 1969)	This picture book is about the friendship of a real mouse Alexander who befriends a wind-up mouse Willy.	The pictures take the form of a collage and are representational in nature. There are little details presented in the pictures, which align with the written text.
Bored Tom (Avi, 2008)	This short story tells the story of Tom who meets a cat while complaining that he is bored.	The story incorporates dialogue and descriptive details.
Good as New (Tapper, 2012)	This *Sport Illustrated for Kids* article discusses the elbow injuries of baseball pitchers.	This article contains content-specific, medical vocabulary and the names of different baseball pitchers and their teams.
Jack y Los Frijoles Mágicos [*Jack and the Beanstalk*] (2012)	This story is part of a collection of fairy and folk tales.	The story is written in conventional Spanish and has very little to no picture support.
かさ *[Umbrella]* (Matsuno, 1985)	This picture book is about different types of umbrellas and the people holding them.	The text is written in Japanese Hiragana and the book uses repetitive sentence structures. The illustrations are not detailed but support the written text.

Title and Author	*Story Synopsis*	*Special Features*
Peanut Butter Rhino (Andriani, 1994)	This picture book is about a rhino who packs a lunch to visit his friend. When the rhino sits on his peanut butter sandwich, he enlists the help of his friends to find it.	This book has repetitive and predictable sentence structures and strong picture support. The text is written in dialogue bubbles to show that the characters are talking with one another.
おつきさまこんばんは *[Good Evening, Moon]* (Hayashi, 1986)	This picture book tells the story of the moon coming up in the evening sky.	The book is written in Japanese Hiragana and has picture support but the illustrations lack visual details.
Small Wonder (Ghosh, 2012)	A *Sports Illustrated for Kids* article featuring the soccer player Lionel Messi.	The format of the article is designed to represent an interview with Messi. The article has content-specific vocabulary.
Spring and *The Story* (Lobel, 2011)	Part of the Frog and Toad series, *Spring* is a short story that describes how the Frog tried to wake up the Toad because spring has arrived. *The Story* is about how Frog asked Toad to tell him a story.	The story has very little illustrations that support the text. The sentences are short and mostly simple sentences.
Straw Maid (Lobel, 1983)	This story is about a young girl who escapes three robbers by making a straw maid to serve in her place.	This book has illustrations, without much details, that support the text. The storyline is modeled after a fable.
Το καλύτερο σκιουράκι του δάσους [The Best Squirrel in the Forest] (Korla, 1975)	This picture book is about a little squirrel who helped an elderly woman, who awarded him by giving him a nut.	This picture book has strong picture support with detailed illustrations and a predictable storyline. It is written in the Greek.
The Garden of Abdul Gasazi (Van Allsburg, 1979)	This picture book tells the story of a boy Alan who chases after his dog to find himself in the garden of the magician Abdul Gasazi.	The storyline has several inferential components. The pictures support the story elements and are in black and white pencil drawings.
Ο λαγός και οι Φίλοι του [The Hare and His Friends] (Aesop, 1995)	An Aesop fable, the story is about a hare who asks his friends to help him when dogs chase after him.	This book has strong picture support and a predictable storyline. It is written in the Greek.

(*Continued*)

Table 1.1 (Continued)

Title and Author	*Story Synopsis*	*Special Features*
The Invention of Hugo Cabret (Selznick, 2007)	This chapter book is a mystery that focuses on Hugo's life. Hugo is an orphan boy and a clockkeeper for the Paris train station.	The story is built around very descriptive language to build details and imaginary.
Ο Ποντικός της Εξοχής και ο ποντικός της Πόλης [The Mouse of the Countryside and the City Mouse] (Aesop, 1995)	An Aesop fable, the story describes the adventures of two cousins when they visit each other in the city and in the countryside.	The book has strong picture support and a predictable storyline. It is written in the Greek alphabet.
うしろにいるのだれ [Who Is Behind Me?] (Fukuda, 2004)	This picture book asks who is behind, under, on top of, and under a variety of animals.	The book is written in Japanese Hiragana. The story uses a repetitive and predictable sentence structure. The illustrations cover two pages and give a clue to the next animal. The text does not include any punctuation marks.
Yo, Naomi Leon (Ryan, 2005)	This chapter book tells the story of a young girl Naomi who reunites with her mother and father after years of separation. This book is a Spanish translation.	The book has descriptive language and centers around character development.
Yo, Vikings (Schachner, 2002)	A picture book that tells the story of Emma, who becomes fascinated and captivated by the Viking Eric the Red.	The book has detailed illustrations that provide support to the written text.

RMA). Family RMA offers retrospective discussions about readers' oral reading and high-quality miscues. Family RMA was a tool that allowed me to create a shared space to construct knowledge with family members about reading. Throughout this book, I will refer to the Family RMA data as reflective and collaborative discussions about bilingual readers' miscues. The subsequent chapters will go into more details on how these data informed the construction of the Profiles.

Concluding Thoughts

Juxtaposing the data from the bilingual families who were part of *Revaluing Readers and Families* with revisiting data from Emma allows new opportunities for diverse voices to be heard through the Profiles. In *Becoming Biliterate*, I wrote,

> There are many challenges that teachers and teacher-educators face today. We face political control, high stakes testing, and top-down curriculum models, and we also face challenges in how we can critically think about our own beliefs and teaching in the classroom. Testing and curricula are negatively changing the ways in which we teach children. Discourses are shifting and identities are being tied to labels such as "reader," "above grade level," and "below grade level." The discussion is not new, but the social and political realities in which these labels are occurring are menacing.

Although 10 years have passed, these ideas still resonate today. As Bomer and Maloch (2012) remind us, "Living things can't really be standardized that way – they require a focus on the local" (p. 44). The Profiles provide a formative manner of assessing readers from a humanistic perspective that positions students as social actors and acknowledges the diversity of meaning as arising out of a dynamic languaging context. The Profiles, as a culturally relevant assessment tool, capture the local knowledge of bilingual readers. Documenting the range of sophisticated ways readers use language and transact with text, the Profiles illustrate how bilingual reading abilities and identities are socially constructed and manifest themselves within home and school literacy practices. The chapters will use the breadth of data to explore each of these purposes through the Profiles. In the next chapter, I will dive further into the Profile sections.

References

Aesop. (1995). *The hare and his friends.* Angyra.

Aesop. (1995). *The mouse of the countryside and the city mouse.* Recos.

Andriani, V. (1994). *Peanut butter rhino.* Scholastic.

Artiles, A. J., Harry, B., Reschly, D. J., & Chinn, P. C. (2002). Over-identification of students of color in special education: A critical overview. *Multicultural Perspectives, 4*(1), 3–10.

Ascenzi-Moreno, L. (2018). Translanguaging and responsive assessment adaptations: Emergent bilingual readers through the lens of possibility. *Language Arts, 95*(6), 355–368.

Avi. (2008). Bored Tom. In *Strange happenings: Five tales of transformation* (pp. 1–32). HMH Books for Young Readers.

Bomer, R., & Maloch, B. (2012). Diverse local literacies and standardizing policies. *Language Arts, 90*(1), 44.

Cody, A. (2014). *The educator and the oligarch: A teacher challenges the Gates Foundation.* Garn Press.

Curdt-Christiansen, X. L. (2009). Invisible and visible language planning: Ideological factors in the family language policy of Chinese immigrant families in Quebec. *Language policy, 8*(4), 351–375.

Curdt-Christiansen, X. L., & La Morgia, F. (2018). Managing heritage language development: Opportunities and challenges for Chinese, Italian and Pakistani Urdu-speaking families in the UK. *Multilingua, 37*(2), 177–200.

Everett, J., Reid, G., & Elbeheri, G. (2013). Assessment approaches for multilingual learners with dyslexia. *Researching Dyslexia in Multilingual Settings*, 18–35.

Freire, P. (2003). *Pedagogy of the oppressed*. Continuum.

Fukuda, T. (2004). *Ushiro ni iru no dare*. Shinpusha.

Gay, G. (2000). *Culturally responsive teaching*. Teachers College Press.

Gee, J. P. (2004). *An introduction to discourse analysis: Theory and method*. Routledge.

Ghosh, B. (2012). Small wonder. *Sports Illustrated for Kids, 24*(3), 50–51.

Goodman, D., Flurkey, A., & Goodman, Y. (2007). Effective young beginning readers. In Y. Goodman & P. Martens (Eds.), *Critical issues in early literacy*. Lawrence Erlbaum.

Goodman, Y., Watson, D., & Burke, C. L. (2005). *Reading miscue inventory: From evaluation to instruction* (2nd ed.). Richard C. Owen.

Harmey, S. (2021). Perspectives on dealing with reading difficulties. *Education 3–13, 49*(1), 52–62.

Hayashi, A. (1986). *Otsukisama konbawa*. Fukuinkan Shoten.

Jack y los frijoles mágicos [*Jack and the Beanstalk*]. (2012). In *365 Cuentos Clásicos, Rimas, Y Otras Historias* [365 classic stories, rhymes, and other stories] (pp. 1–4). Parragon Books.

Kabuto, B. (2009). Parents and children reading together: The possibilities of Family RMA. *The Reading Teacher, 63*(3), 212–223.

Kabuto, B. (Ed.). (2017). *Teaching without testing: Assessing the complexity of children's literacy learning* (D. Taylor, Ed.). Garn Press Women Scholars Series Volume 2. Garn Press.

Kim, G. M. (2020). Challenging native speakerism in literacy research and education. *Journal of Literacy Research, 52*(3), 368–375.

Korla. (1975). *The best squirrel in the forest*. Angyra.

Kristeva, J. (2003). Stranger to ourselves. In International Center for Photography (Ed.), *Strangers: The first ICP triennial of photography and video*. Steidl.

Lionni, L. (1969). *Alexander and the wind-up mouse*. Dragonfly Books.

Lobel, A. (1983). *Straw maid*. Greenwillow Books.

Lobel, A. (2011). Spring. In *Frog and toad are friends* (pp. 4–15). Harper Collins.

Lobel, A. (2011). The story. In *Frog and toad are friends* (pp. 16–27). Harper Collins.

Macías, R. F. (2016). Language ideologies and rhetorical structures in bilingual education policy and research: Richard Ruiz's 1984 discursive turn. *Bilingual Research Journal, 39*(3–4), 173–199.

Manyak, P., & Dantas, M. L. (2010). Introduction. In M. L. Dantas & P. Manyak (Eds.), *Home- school connections in a multicultural society: Learning from and with culturally and linguistically diverse families* (pp. 1–14). Routledge.

Matsuno, M. (1985). *Kasa*. Fukuinkan Shoten.

National Research Council. (2001). *Knowing what students know: The science and design of educational assessment*. National Academies Press.

Oluo, I. (2019). *So you want to talk about race*. Hachette Book Group.

Pierce, K. M., & Ordoñez-Jasis, R. (2018). *Going public with assessment: A community practice approach*. National Council of Teachers of English.

Ren, L., & Hu, G. (2013). Prolepsis, syncretism, and synergy in early language and literacy practices: A case study of family language policy in Singapore. *Language policy, 12*(1), 63–82.

Rueda, R., & Windmueller, M. P. (2006). English language learners, LD, and overrepresentation: A multiple-level analysis. *Journal of Learning Disabilities, 39*(2), 99–107.
Ryan, P. M. (2005). *Yo, Naomi Leon* (N. Molinero, Trans.). Scholastic en Espanol.
Sanchez, S. V., Rodriguez, B. J., Soto-Huerta, M. E., Villarreal, F. C., Guerra, N. S., & Flores, B. B. (2013). A case for multidimensional bilingual assessment. *Language Assessment Quarterly, 10*(2), 160–177.
Sato, W. (1995). *Ahiru no Tamago*. Fukuinkan-Shoten.
Schachner, J. B. (2002). *Yo, Vikings!* Dutton Children's Books.
Selznick, B. (2007). *The invention of Hugo Cabret*. Scholastic.
Tapper, C. (2012). Good as new. *Sports Illustrated for Kids, 24*(4), 42–45.
Van Allsburg, C. (1979). *The garden of Abdul Gasazi*. HMH Books for Young Readers.
Vanlommel, K., & Schildkamp, K. (2019). How do teachers make sense of data in the context of high-stakes decision making? *American Educational Research Journal, 56*(3), 792–821.
Whitehead, A. N. (1925). *Science and the modern world*. The Free Press.
Willis, A. I. (2019). Race, response to intervention, and reading research. *Journal of Literacy Research, 51*(4), 394–419.

2 Laying the Groundwork for Biographic Biliteracy Profiles

Thomas expressed confidence in his reading when reading diverse texts, and said that he likes to read materials, particularly books, in Spanish or English. Thomas noted that the amount of reading English materials has increased while reading in Spanish materials has decreased. He said that if he could spend more time reading, he would like to improve his reading in Spanish because, as Thomas said, "Since I have been doing a lot of English, I would like to learn the language that my grandmother talks . . . Spanish."

Thomas noted that one of the challenges of reading more Spanish materials is the lack of access to them. He said that he mostly reads materials in English at home. To provide her children with more Spanish reading materials, Maria took them to the public library near Thomas's school on their way home.

This excerpt comes from Thomas's Profile and captures a moment of trying to understand Thomas as a bilingual reader (Appendix B provides Thomas's complete Profile). As this short excerpt illustrates, the purpose of the Profile is to capture a student's learning biography, defined as a constructed narrative built from small stories (Bamberg & Georgakopoulou, 2008) that reveal the complex ways that bilingual reading behaviors are fashioned as part of a reader's social, cultural, and linguistic worlds. Thomas's excerpt, for example, presents an instance when, in describing his reading behaviors, he explained himself as a reader through the linguistic diversity of his family and access to materials within the home and community.

Thomas's mother Maria had aspirations for her children to be bilingual and biliterate. Toward that end, she consciously engaged in a variety of social activities at home to support her aspirations. Maria read to Thomas and Jenny every night when they were younger, although, as Maria noted, bedtime reading was not part of Ecuadorian culture. She, however, adopted the practice when Thomas's kindergarten teacher recommended it. Thomas said that his mother reading to him was important to him in learning how to read. When Thomas got older, he, in turn, read to his little sister Jenny. When it was time for Thomas to start school,

DOI: 10.4324/9781003045984-3

Maria decided to send Thomas to a dual-language school one hour by train from her house.

Maria's language planning and the transgenerational nature in which her children's literacy behaviors were developed through the family were particularly striking in his comment, "Since I have been doing a lot of English, I would like to learn the language that my grandmother talks . . . Spanish." With a family whose mother took great risks to come to the United States due to an uncertain immigration status, Thomas has never met his grandparents and the likelihood of that happening was quite slim. And yet, the connections between language and family defined who Thomas was as a reader and who he wanted to be within his learning biography.

In this chapter, I will provide a framework for the Profiles. Table 2.1 provides a general outline of the Profiles; there are three distinct areas that

Table 2.1 Outline Used for the Biographic Biliteracy Profiles

Section	*Description*
Learning Biography	**Observe and discuss the following over different time periods and contexts:**
	What are the readers' and families' learning backgrounds and histories?
	What interests do the readers have? What types of activities do the families engage in?
	What kinds of reading and writing do they like to do outside of school?
	What topics or themes are the readers interested in?
	**How do readers define a "good" reader in X language? And Y language?*
	**What do readers think it would take to get better at reading in X? And in Y?*
Observations of a Reader	**Observe and discuss the following over different time periods and contexts:**
	Ask readers to choose and read different types of texts and record their oral reading behaviors.
	What types of miscues do they make in X language? And Y language?
	What are their patterns of miscues in each language or for each text?
	How do they use different modes (i.e., written text, pictures, illustration, etc.) to construct meaning?
	Do they monitor their reading for meaning in each language or for each text? If so, how?
	How do they use discursive language practices to retell stories?
	Over time, observe and discuss the following:
	What behaviors did you notice?
	***What behaviors were new?*
	***What has stayed the same?*
	***What is different?*
	How do these behaviors support or challenge the reader's learning biography?

Section	*Description*
Biliteracy Manifestations	**Conclude and discuss the following:** *What do your observations tell you about readers as bilingual readers?* *How are the learning biographies supported or challenged by your observations?* *What types of diverse, real-world practices connect to the readers' identities as evidenced by their learning biographies and your observations?*

Source: Adapted from Kabuto and Harmey (2020).

* See Burke Reading Interview in Goodman et al. (2005).
** From Harmey (2015).

will provide a map for discussing bilingual readers and their reading behaviors in this book. Bilingual reading behaviors represent a range of actions, words, patterns of language use, and feelings that are connected to reading text. These reading behaviors include not only observations and analysis of how students orally read and retell texts but also the language patterns and linguistic moves that arise from those oral readings and retellings. Linguistically diverse reading behaviors are also situated and act in tandem with the social context from which they originate. Gee (2002) wrote,

> If someone wants to know about the development of literacy, he or she should not ask how literacy and language develop. Rather, he or she should ask how a specific set of sociocultural practices (or sets of them) embedded in specific ways with printed words develops.
>
> (p. 31)

Gee (1996) noted that the analysis of sociocultural practices considers the who (i.e., the participants engaging in activities) as well as the what (i.e., what the participants are doing). In this vein, bilingual reading behaviors arise from the social and cultural practices that draw on those types of behaviors to make actions and interactions happen.

To define bilingual reading behaviors as linguistic actions that arise from social and cultural practices, I will first discuss learning biographies as learning histories within family and school contexts. Then, I will present how bilingual reading behaviors, as the observable act of orally reading and retelling text, are viewed from a socio-psycholinguistic perspective on reading. In particular, the addition of a translanguaging lens will add to the understanding of how reading as a language process is a unified process regardless of the forms that compose the named languages. Finally, I will discuss the last part of the Profile, biliteracy manifestations. This section will explore how linguistically diverse reading behaviors result from not only a social and cultural context but also a translanguaging context.

Learning Biographies Within Profiles

A biography involves telling a life story, whether our own through personal biographies or autobiographies or that of another. A learning biography, therefore, integrates students' learning histories, current learning trajectories, and future learning potentials into their life stories. Learning biographies provide glimpses into readers' identity enactments, or how one fashions and authors a sense of who they are in relation to other people, places, and things through the telling of stories and narratives (Coffey & Street, 2008).

Profiles are thus considered what Bakhtin termed dialogic, or multivoiced (Holquist, 1981), as the voices of two tellers come together: one the biographer's and the other is that of the subject of the biography. I will use the term biographer in this chapter as a neutral term to denote any individual (teacher, researcher, literacy coach, etc.) who may be engaged in the writing of a Profile. In this book, for instance, the Profiles represent partially my voice and perspectives as well as those I tried to capture and coordinate through various storylines that emerged from the data to create a larger narrative of what it means to be a bilingual reader in becoming biliterate. In this way, each Profile is unique and tells a distinct story of the teller, partly because, as Ochs and Capps (1996) remind us, "the tale . . . lies beyond the telling." Thomas's symbolic connection to his grandmother, whom he had not yet had the opportunity to meet, exemplifies, in what may seem like a passing comment in a very brief moment, how deep insight into the social and emotional driving forces for language learning can come to the fore.

In other words, the tale of Thomas's identity as a bilingual reader was intertwined with social and emotional factors embedded in his family's history. Thomas's statement about his grandmother took his thoughts and feelings and formed them into something real and tangible in how he saw himself in the context of his family. A biographer's role is to be a close observer who not only "captures a brief glimpse of the complexity of the symbol-weaving that takes place in the problem-solving situations as children reconstruct the functions, uses, and forms of written language" (Taylor in Kabuto, 2017, p. 90) but also takes on the role of an informed listener who documents how language serves multiple communicative functions to represent students' versions of their realities. Biographers organize narratives around past and present events with future possibilities.

Narratives and Language

In educational research, the term *narrative* is defined broadly to mean, on one end of spectrum, how one tells a story using story patterns and, at the other end of spectrum, the construction of larger patterns of meaning formed from socially situated actions and identity performances (Mishler, 1999). The former sees narratives and stories similarly while the latter views them differently. The learning biographies encountered in this book result from narratives that are constructed from storied realities based on students' experiences. Constructing narratives is a means of organizing and making sense of the multiple and varied experiences that result from the stories, large or small, that we tell (Cronon, 1992).

Stories, on the other hand, are viewed as the oral and written storylines that individuals produce based on their experiences. Rogers (2004) used the term *storied selves* to describe how individuals develop understandings of themselves and their identities through stories. Bamberg and Georgakopoulou (2008) expanded this idea to describe "small stories" that are told in the fleeting moments of engaging in activities (p. 123). The idea of small stories plays a critical role in the development of narratives that inform the learning biographies in the Profiles. Thomas's statement about his grandmother is an example of a small story. In the time I spent with Thomas, he told other small stories like that of his three dogs, his exhaustion from taking the state tests, and reading to his sister Jenny at home. Bamberg and Georgakopoulou (2008) suggested that small stories live "on the fringes of narrative research" (p. 1).

In the construction of learning biographies, biographers move these stories from the fringes to the heart of understanding the identity of linguistically diverse readers. This movement requires focusing on the "teller's representations of past events, and how the tellers make sense of themselves in light of these past events" (Bamberg & Georgakopoulou, 2008, p. 1). Biographers do not just retell these stories – they connect the multiple storylines in various ways to form a narrative that challenges deficit-oriented perspectives of linguistic diversity that devalue certain types of language practices in home or school.

The learning biographies that undergird the Profiles are the first step in creating culturally responsive ways to understand what students know and how that knowledge is directly or indirectly connected to readers' linguistic, social, and cultural experiences. Learning biographies situate learning experiences and reading behaviors within an asset-oriented narrative that brings their small stories into meaningful storylines connected to their social and cultural lives.

Observations of a Reader: Defining Linguistically Diverse Reading Behaviors

Thomas conducted six oral readings and retellings: one short story (Bored Tom), two Sports Illustrated for Kids articles, and three chapters in the book Yo, Naomi Leon (see Table 1.2). The oral readings and retellings occurred in a translanguaging context. In some sessions, Thomas read texts written in Spanish, like Yo, Noami Leon, and in English, like the articles from Sports Illustrated for Kids. In two of the three oral readings and retelling sessions for Yo, Noami Leon, Thomas retold the story in English. There were also sessions in which Thomas discussed his reading patterns and miscues for Yo, Naomi Leon, in English.

When reading, 90% (or more) of the sentences Thomas read were grammatically acceptable. The semantic acceptability of his sentences (i.e., whether they made sense) ranged from 79% when reading Good as New to 99% when reading Chapter 3 of Yo, Naomi Leon. Thomas demonstrated an understanding of the texts that he read. After reading Small Wonder, for instance, Thomas described the story, saying:

> *It was talking about what he [Messi] does when he plays soccer. He says what he does [and] about his childhood. When he was little and he practiced and that's why he's a professional football player. Every time he loses, he feels bad for himself. He doesn't scream or stuff like that. He also talks about how he gets prepared for the 2014 World Cup.*

When he read Chapter 3 of Yo, Naomi Leon, Thomas retold the chapter as:

> *This chapter was about Naomi and Owen and the grandmother talking about Naomi's mother. Naomi noticed that the grandmother would worry about the mother. I think that the grandmother was worried because the mother might take Naomi and Owen away from her to a different place. Since the day that the mother came, the grandmother was not the same. She was different. Her attitude was different.*

In the Profiles, the observations of the readers attempt to capture a glimpse of readers' bilingual reading behaviors through close observations, documentation, and analysis of the readers' oral readings and retellings, as well as accompanying dialogue. Observing bilingual reading behaviors in this way is viewed through a socio-psycholinguistic perspective of reading.

Coined and founded by Ken Goodman (1996), socio-psycholinguistic theory views reading as a constructive meaning-making process. The reading process is seen as a social process, in which readers draw from their language experiences, as well as a linguistic one. As a linguistic process, readers use language cueing systems (also described as linguistic cueing systems), defined as the syntactic (or grammatical), the semantic (or meaning), and the graphophonic systems. Finally, readers employ psycholinguistic strategies, also referred to as reading strategies, which are (a) initiate, sample, and select – the strategy that describes how readers focus on and select from information in the text (i.e., graphophonic, grammar, meaning, or picture); (b) predict and infer – the strategy that describes how readers predict upcoming text and ideas; (c) confirm, disconfirm, and correct – the strategy that describes how readers confirm or disconfirm their predictions and correct them based on whether their predictions make sense; (d) integrate – the strategy by which readers integrate predicted knowledge into their current schema; and (e) terminate – the strategy by which readers select when and where to stop reading.

Through socio-psycholinguistic theory, Goodman argued that miscues – responses readers produce that differ from the written text – are windows into the language cues and reading strategies that readers employ when they read. As Goodman suggested, while we cannot enter the heads of our readers, we can analyze readers' miscues to better understand how they transact with text using the reading process. To provide an illustration, consider the following sentence that Thomas read from *Small Wonder* (Ghosh, 2012): "I never really fixated on him or compared myself ***to*** another player" (p. 51). Thomas substituted to with the word ***with*** to read the sentence as, "I never really fixated on him or compared myself ***with*** another player." In this example, Thomas used the syntactic cueing system to substitute a word that maintained the grammatical structure of the sentence. At the same time, he used the semantic cueing system to produce a word that would make sense. In other words, the miscue substitution was grammatically acceptable and meaningful in the sentence.

When considering psycholinguistic reading strategies, Thomas was most likely predicting based on grammar and his familiarity with language. When he read the sentence as, "I never really fixated on him or compared myself ***with*** another player," he confirmed that the sentence made sense, which caused him to continue reading during our reflective discussions of his miscue.

Thomas exhibited a similar type of pattern when he read *Yo, Naomi Leon* (Ryan, 2005). When Thomas read the sentence, "Era ***el*** nino más redondo de la escuela Buena Vista y uno de los más simpáticos" (He was the roundest child at Buena Vista school and one of the friendliest), he substituted ***el*** for ***un***. Thomas's produced sentence read, "Era ***un*** nino más redondo de la escuela Buena Vista y uno de los más simpáticos" (He was a rounder boy from Buena Vista school and one of the friendliest). In this example, Thomas used the grammatical cueing system to substitute ***el*** with ***un***. Drawing from the semantic cueing system, Thomas created a substitution that would also make sense. Thomas was most likely predicting as he read and used the syntactic and semantic cueing systems to produce a miscue that was both grammatically acceptable and made sense. Because of this, Thomas confirmed his prediction.

These two examples illustrate how viewing oral reading behaviors through socio-psycholinguistic theory suggests that reading is a process of active meaning construction as readers transact with the surface features of language to create a deeper meaning. The surface structure consists of the observable characteristics of written language, or the physical and measurable aspects (Smith, 2012). In both examples, Thomas attended to the graphic features of both texts. He, however, used them in an efficient manner as he constructed a deeper meaning of the text (Smith, 2012). This deep meaning cannot be directly measured or observed and was what guided Thomas's understanding, allowing him to make meaningful predictions based on his knowledge of grammar and meaningful sentence structures. In other words, when Thomas made the word substitutions (***with*** for ***to*** and ***un*** for ***el***), he was predicting based on grammar and meaning and did not necessarily need to overly focus on the graphic features.

Reading as a Unified Language Process

The research on translanguaging adds another dimension to understanding bilingual reading behaviors. Translanguaging views language as a unified linguistic repertoire (Garcia & Wei, 2014). Connecting this view of language from a socio-psycholinguistic perspective to the study of linguistically diverse reading behaviors highlights how reading is a universal process, or a unified language process. Goodman (1996) wrote about the universality of reading, "In spite of the diversity within, reading is a universal process, a single way of making sense of written language" (p. 9). In other words, regardless of the syntactic and semantic features and graphic forms that make up written language systems, readers draw upon a range of linguistic features within a language or across languages to demonstrate their understandings of and construct meaning with written text.

Taking this perspective suggests that bilingual reading behaviors are not just the interaction and influence of one linguistic system, say Spanish, with another linguistic system, like English. Deep meaning is not necessarily observable, tangible, and translatable through the surface features of named languages. Evidence of this came from Thomas's retellings and the reflective discussions of his miscues. In the opening section, I presented Thomas's retelling of Chapter 3 of *Yo, Naomi Leon*. Thomas read aloud Chapter 3 of the book, which was written in Spanish. After he read, Livia asked him to retell the chapter, which he did in English. This retelling discussion resulted:

"So tell me, what was this all about?," Livia asked.

Thomas said, "This chapter was about Naomi and Owen and the grandmother talking about Naomi's mother. Naomi noticed that the grandmother would worry about the mother."

"And why do you think the grandmother was worried?"

"I think that the grandmother was worried because the mother might take Naomi and Owen away from her to a different place," Thomas replied.

Livia asked, "Ok, did it say that in the chapter?"

"No."

Livia added, "But you are thinking that that might happen. Do you think that the kids were worried? What do you think the kids were thinking?"

Thomas responded, "I think Naomi was worried, but Owen not that much."

"Why do you think that Naomi thought it was strange for her grandmother to behave the way she was behaving?"

"Because since the day that the mother came, the grandmother was not the same. She was different. Her attitude was different," Thomas explained.

"And what happened at the end that was so catastrophic?," Livia asked.
"They were going to miss an episode of Wheel of Fortune."
"How many episodes had they watched all together?
Thomas said, "In total, 743."

Thomas provided a retelling that demonstrated his understanding of the chapter. His retelling included details, like the number of episodes of Wheel of Fortune that Naomi and her grandmother had watched together and a discussion of the overall character changes that Naomi saw in her grandmother. Notably, the language of the text and the retelling, while taking different linguistic forms, did not result in barriers to Thomas's ability to demonstrate his understanding of the text. The fluidity of the language context supported a translanguaging perspective so that bilinguals are not balancing two separate linguistic systems. Rather, bilingual readers like Thomas draw on a range of language forms for communicative and meaningful purposes to transact not only with the text but also with others who participate in the reading context.

This type of dynamic language behavior was also evident in our reflective discussions about Thomas's miscues. During one of our sessions, Thomas read the sentence from *Yo, Naomi Leon* (Ryan, 2005), "Naomi fue a ***un psicólogo*** durante dos años" [Naomi went to a psychologist for two years] (p. 25) as "Naomi fue a ***una psicóloga*** durante dos años." Thomas substituted the feminine for the masculine form of the word psychologist (*un/a psicólogo/a*). During one of our reflective conversations on whether Thomas's miscues made sense, Livia showed him the substitution and the following dialogue emerged:

Livia said, "Did you hear what you did? What did you do?"
Thomas replied, "I said una psicóloga." [a female psychologist]
Livia clarified how the text should read, "And what is it?"
"Un psicólogo." [a male psychologist]
Livia turned to Maria and said in Spanish, "Thomas said psychologist (feminine form), but its psychologist (masculine form). He did the same thing three times."
Livia said to Thomas in English, "Three times, Thomas, you did the same thing. So why do you think you did that?"
"I'm not sure."
"Because when I asked you to read it, you said una psicóloga – a psychologist (female),"
Livia said. "Then I asked you to read it again and you said una psicóloga – a psychologist. Then, when you heard it, I don't think you caught it. Did you catch it when you heard it [on the tape]?"
"No."
Livia asked, "Do you think that it makes a difference whether you say una psicóloga [female psychologist], or un psicólogo [male psychologist]?"

"No, not really. The only difference is that they change the O and the A [for feminine and masculine]," Thomas replied.
"It says that the girl visited a psychologist."
Thomas explained, "I was thinking that the psychologist is a woman and not a man."

In this example, Thomas, Livia, and Maria discussed Thomas's miscue and the written text within a dynamic language context as they moved between the written language of the text and the spoken languages of the participants. In this one particular collaborative discussion, Thomas discussed how his miscue was the result of a change in graphic information, but the change did not inherently disrupt the meaning that Thomas constructed as he read. Thomas predicted that the psychologist was a woman, which then caused him to read the feminine form of the word.

These examples illustrate how translanguaging is not just the language norm – it also provides a context, or space (Wei, 2011), for Thomas, Maria, and Livia to generate shared knowledge of each other as bilingual readers. The context, while made up of people and things, maintained a dynamic state through language fluidity, as defined from a translanguaging perspective. In order for there to be a translanguaging context, a variety of linguistic forms must be present from which participants may freely select. For instance, even within the fluidity of the language context, Thomas talked about "Spanish" and "English" forms. For Thomas, these forms were not without value and meaning.

The selection of linguistic forms and movement among them can be viewed from a code-switching perspective, which I will take the liberty to redefine as moving among a range of linguistic resources, including but not limited to linguistic oral and written forms and meaning and semiotic systems. Bypassing a definition of code-switching that limits its understanding to switching among codes as isolated linguistic units, which some researchers support and advocate, means recentering meaning at the heart of why individuals may draw from a range of linguistic resources within a translanguaging context. Pennycook (2010) argued, "Issues of language diversity will be crucial, especially if we attempt to step away from a view of diversity in terms of enumerating languages, and instead focus on diversity of meaning. The ways in which languages can be understood multimodally, as working in different modes in different domains, will also be significant" (p. 3). These ideas will be further explored in more detail in Chapter 4.

Biliteracy Manifestations Within a Translanguaging Context

The construction of Thomas's Profile resulted from interviews with Thomas, oral reading, and retelling events with diverse texts, and reflective and collaborative discussions of Thomas's miscues. These artifacts, or manifestations, illustrate the complex ways that

> *his reading behaviors were part and parcel of the linguistic diversity of the family, school and local contexts within which reading was situated. At the beginning of the sessions, Thomas expressed his confidence in reading diverse texts and within contexts that lacked language barriers and differentiation. The reading data from the miscue analyses support that Thomas was not only comfortable in orally reading and retelling texts presented to him. He was also reflective on his miscues when reading diverse texts, why he made them, and how the discussions changed him as a reader. In the process of reading diverse texts, Thomas enacted effective bilingual reading behaviors and was reflective of himself as a linguistically diverse reader. When asked about reading the diverse texts that were part of the reflective conversations, Thomas responded that he did not feel that he did anything different when reading texts written in Spanish and English. Thomas said, "When I read in English or in Spanish, if I make a mistake I go back to the sentence and make sure that the sentence makes sense."*

The concept of biliteracy manifestations draws from the work of Whitmore and Meyer (2020) to describe the "demonstrations of meaning making," or 'stuff,' that arise out of the meaning-making process, including but not limited to reading and writing and learners' thought processes. Literacy manifestations are affective, situated in sociocultural and linguistic contexts, and sensitive to time (Whitmore & Meyer, 2020).

As discussed in the previous excerpt, reading, as a demonstration of meaning construction, manifested itself within family and school practices. For Thomas, being a bilingual reader was just as much about connecting to the text as it was about bonding with family to recreate in-the-moment feelings and connections to reading. In other words, Thomas's bilingual reading behaviors had a symbolic and local aspect as they were also rooted in his family and the actual and imagined (like his grandmother) shared histories. Literacy manifestations, therefore, are the evidence of reading events and practices that are connected to home and school contexts, diverse places, and people. These manifestations resulted from Thomas's identity enactments, or how he used language to create a self-in-practice. This self-in-practice was only possible because it was embedded in the sociocultural and linguistic contexts framed by translanguaging.

By "context," I refer to a general definition of shared spaces, places, and locations. Through this definition, context can be demarcated by certain physical boundaries and locations, like a school building, or it can be fluid, dynamic open spaces defined by the people and things in that shared space. For instance, literacy research has a long history of exploring schools, in the broadest sense, and classrooms as physical and metaphorical borders that privilege certain ways of using language and demonstrating knowledge. When students are removed from the physical boundaries of schools and observed in their home or work contexts, what they know and how they communicate that knowledge suddenly changes (Gonzalez et al., 2005). Students who have been seen as underachieving were then perceived as knowledgeable experts in a context outside of school.

A more nuanced and multifaceted definition of context needs to be considered. This definition draws from the dialogical and constructive nature of context in that there are not only people, things, and ways of acting and being that help to define the context. There are also unseen aspects that can influence and often undergird how individuals within that shared space act and participate in practice. These unseen social processes connect to ideologies, status, and power relations, which can privilege or limit particular ways of acting and being in any context.

For linguistically diverse students, as illustrated in Thomas's Profile, their literacy manifestations are often constructed within a translanguaging context. Similar to any context, a translanguaging context is conceptualized and realized through social activities and processes. In addition, whether the context refers to a classroom, church, restaurant, or store, language plays a role in organizing activities. As such, researchers suggest that we need to move away from thinking of language as a closed structure and system to one of doing, or languaging (Pennycook, 2010).

Unique to itself, a translanguaging context allows for the fluidity of language use, or as Pennycook described, the remaking of language. Pennycook (2010) explained, "We remake the language and the space in which this happens." (p. 2). How language forms are used, come together, negotiated, valued, and sometimes devalued are the result of how individuals or groups of individuals interpret the translanguaging context. At the same time, how individuals respond and use language to engage in activity reinforces how they identify the context. For instance, Thomas was able to use translanguaging practices because the context, defined by the materials (like books) and people (like Maria, Livia, and me), supported and valued the practice. In turn, as Thomas interpreted each session, reading event, and collaborative discussion over time, translanguaging then reinforced the context in which those social activities were embedded. The result was that Thomas was able to demonstrate and articulate his sense making and thought processes and produce artifacts that are windows into literacy identities (Whitmore & Meyer, 2020).

Identity is a concept built on collective aspects of personal and social selves (Hannover & Zander, 2020; Silseth & Arnseth, 2011). Identity is thus lived through and located within social practices, as much as it is a product of a translanguaging context for linguistically diverse readers. In Chapter 5, I will conceptualize identity through two interrelated concepts – the self-in-action and the sense-of-self – and discuss how these two interrelated views inform the process of becoming not just a bilingual reader but also in becoming biliterate.

Concluding Thoughts

Through the concept of learning biographies, observations of readers, and biliteracy manifestations, the Profiles illustrate the complexity of becoming biliterate. The Profiles provide an integrative and interdisciplinary means of understanding the connections between identity, becoming a bilingual reader, and biliteracy. The subsequent chapters focus more on the examination of the translanguaging context of the readers in this book. In Chapter 3, we will meet Mai and Sophie to study the reading process as a unified process for reading texts written in other written language systems. Chapter 3 also takes a closer look at the miscues and comprehension of these two readers within a translanguaging context. Chapters 3 through 5 conclude with lessons learned from the themes that connect the Profiles.

References

Bamberg, M., & Georgakopoulou, A. (2008). Small stories as a new perspective in narrative and identity analysis. *Text & Talk – An Interdisciplinary Journal of Language, Discourse Communication Studies, 28*(3), 377–396.

Coffey, S., & Street, B. (2008). Narrative and identity in the "Language Learning Project". *The Modern Language Journal, 92*(3), 452–464.

Cronon, W. (1992). A place for stories: Nature, history, and narrative. *Journal of American History, 78*, 1347–1376.

Garcia, O., & Wei, L. (2014). *Translanguaging: Language, bilingualism, and education*. Palgrave MacMillan.

Gee, J. (1996). *Social linguistics and literacies: Ideology and discourse* (2nd ed.). Routledge-Falmer.

Gee, J. (2002). A sociocultural perspective on early literacy development. In S. Neuman & D. Dickinson (Eds.), *Handbook of early literacy research* (pp. 30–42). Guilford Press.

Ghosh, B. (2012). Small wonder. *Sports Illustrated for Kids, 24*(3), 50–51.

Gonzalez, N., Moll, L., & Amanti, C. (2005). Introduction. In N. Gonzalez, L. Moll, & C. Amanti (Eds.), *Funds of knowledge: Theorizing practices in households, communities, and classroom* (pp. 1–28). Lawrence Erlbaum.

Goodman, K. (1996). *On reading*. Heinemann.

Goodman, Y., Watson, D., & Burke, C. L. (2005). *Reading miscue inventory: From evaluation to instruction* (2nd ed.). Richard C. Owen.

Hannover, B., & Zander, L. (2020). How personal and social selves influence the development of children and adolescents at school. *Zeitschrift Fur Padagogische Psychologie, 34*(2), 65–85.

Harmey, S. (2015). *Change over time in children's co-constructed writing* (Electronic Thesis or Dissertation). Retrieved from http://rave.ohiolink.edu/etdc/view?acc_num=osu1440059434

Holquist, M. (Ed.). (1981). *The dialogic imagination: Four essays by M.M. Bakhtin*. University of Texas Press.

Kabuto, B. (Ed.). (2017). *Teaching without testing: Assessing the complexity of children's literacy learning* (D. Taylor, Ed.). Garn Press Women Scholars Series Volume 2. Garn Press.

Kabuto, B., & Harmey, S. (2020). Documenting the manifestations of learning with the Biographic Literacy Profile. In R. Meyer & K. Whitmore (Eds.), *Reclaiming literacies as meaning making: Manifestations of values, identities, relationships, and knowledge* (pp. 64–74). Routledge.

Mishler, E. (1999). *Storylines: Craftartists' narratives of identity*. Harvard University Press.

Ochs, E., & Capps, L. (1996). Narrating the self. *Annual Review in Anthropology, 25*, 19–43.

Pennycook, A. (2010). *Language as local practice*. Routledge.

Rogers, R. (2004). Storied selves: A critical discourse analysis of adult learners' literate lives. *Reading Research Quarterly*, *39*(3), 272–305.

Ryan, P. M. (2005). *Yo, Naomi Leon* (N. Molinero, Trans.). Scholastic en Espanol.

Silseth, K., & Arnseth, H. C. (2011). Learning and identity construction across sites: A dialogical approach to analyzing the construction of learning selves. *Culture & Psychology*, *17*(1), 65–80.

Smith, F. (2012). *Understanding reading: A psycholinguistic analysis of reading and learning to read*. Routledge.

Wei, L. (2011). Moment analysis and translanguaging space: Discursive construction of identities by multilingual Chinese youth in Britain. *Journal of Pragmatics*, *43*(5), 1222–1235.

Whitmore, K. F., & Meyer, R. J. (2020). Reclaiming manifestations of literacies. In R. J. Meyer & K. F. Whitmore (Eds.), *Reclaiming literacies as meaning making: Manifestations of values, identities, relationships, and knowledge* (pp. 1–18). Routledge.

3 Profiles of Reading in a Translanguaging Context

Bilingual reading behaviors, from a socio-psycholinguistic perspective on reading, evolve from a process of meaning construction. Positioning language as a meaning-centric system untangles how bilingual reading behaviors can both be shaped by and evolve within a translanguaging context. In this chapter, I will focus on Sophie's and Mai's Profiles to explore further a series of reading events. While Thomas provided an example of a reader reading English and Spanish texts, Sophie's and Mai's Profiles present opportunities to study bilingual readers reading texts in different writing systems – Greek and Japanese. In particular, the discussion in this chapter derived from observations of Sophie and Mai as readers to illustrate how their miscues, retellings, and reflective discussions about their miscues created complex pictures of them as bilingual readers.

Miscues and Comprehension of Bilingual Readers

Regardless of the diversity within written languages, socio-psycholinguistic theory offers one common way to discuss bilingual reading behaviors through the analysis of readers' miscues, defined as produced responses to text that differ from the expected responses (Goodman, 1996) and their comprehension. Drawing from the work of Garcia and Wei (2014), research on translanguaging supports the view of the reading process as a universal process without specific processes distinct to writing systems. The reading process, in other words, like translanguaging, transcends language boundaries so that "difference and sameness occur in an apparently impossible simultaneity" (Garcia & Wei, 2014, p. 21). As such, differences in writing systems are not inherent difficulties for bilingual readers. In fact, bilingual readers become metacognitive and aware of themselves as readers, of language forms and structures within writing systems, and of the reading process (Kabuto, 2015, 2017; Wang, 2021; Wang & Gilles, 2017).

Approaching reading as a unified reading process of meaning-making draws from several premises. The first is that there are certain universal characteristics to written language. A written language draws from characteristics that define a writing system, whether it is English, Japanese, Spanish, or Greek, and all writing systems use graphic forms to represent sounds (phonemes),

DOI: 10.4324/9781003045984-4

meanings (morphemes), syllables, or a combination of the three, as in Japanese. In addition, written language is organized by a grammatical structure that helps communicate a message or meaning (Rogers, 2005; Verhoeven & Perfetti, 2017). When grammar is disrupted, for instance, it may be difficult to predict the who, what, when, where, and why of a message. Table 3.1 provides an outline of the writing system features of Greek and Japanese.

Table 3.1 Features of the Greek and Japanese Writing Systems

Writing Systems		
Features	*Greek*	*Japanese*
Writing System Classification	Phonetic (phonemes)	Syllabic (syllable-based) and morpheme (pictures or ideas-based)
Written Forms	Greek alphabet 24 letters in the modern Greek alphabet Both uppercase and lowercase forms (Verhoeven & Perfetti, 2017)	Two kana forms (Hiragana and Katakana): 105 kana forms Kanji: 1,006 Kanji with 2,005 pronunciations Roman alphabet (Kado, 2017)
Orthography (system of spellings)	Ambiguous orthographic system with several ways to spell certain sounds and individual sounds Consist of both vowels and consonants (Verhoeven & Perfetti, 2017)	Shallow orthographic system with a relatively direct relationship with the Japanese sound system and the system of spellings in the language Consist of both vowels and consonants
Writing Directionality	Left to right Word spacing present	Left to right when writing horizontally Top to bottom when writing vertically Word spacing not used
Internal Structure (grammatical organization)	Subject, verb, and object order Prepositions precede the noun phrase. Has an inflectional morphology and inflections are used for nouns and adjectives to represent gender (masculine, feminine, and neuter) and number (singular and plural) (Verhoeven & Perfetti, 2017)	Ambiguous grammatical structure subject–object–verb order delineated by particles The subject of the sentence may be absent if it can be inferred from the context of the sentence Number and verb agreement are not present in the Japanese language Regular use of suffixes in verb formations to change verbs to present, past, and future tenses, as well as representing negative tenses and conditionality Verb suffixes can communicate a formality Suffixes are used to change the part of speech of words, such as transform an adjective to a noun. (Kado, 2017)

While there are adhesive characteristics in writing systems needed to form meaningful text, written language is inherently ambiguous (Goodman, 2011). The second premise relates to this point and suggests that readers are adept at working within the ambiguity of written language as readers use language cues – syntactic, semantic, and graphophonic – and psycholinguistic strategies – sampling, predicting, confirming, and correcting – to make sense of text. In a study of readers reading *Alexander and the Wind-Up Mouse*, I examined the repeated miscue for *wind* (Kabuto, 2014). The word by itself is ambiguous in that it has two pronunciations: *wind* as the "wind blows" or *wind* as in the "wind-up mouse." The majority of readers in the study did not have difficulty disambiguating the word when it occurred in a grammatical and meaningful sentence. In addition, some readers who miscued on *wind* still understood and explained the concept of a wind-up toy and, in the story, Willy was such a toy.

In another example of Japanese, the form は (ha) can be pronounced in two ways depending on its function in the sentence. In its expected phonetic form, it is pronounced as /ha/ as in the word はな (hana, flower). When it appears as a particle, however, it serves the function of a subject marker and is pronounced /wa/ as in "へやへ はいった ばばばあちゃん**は**、 すぐに べっどにすわりこんでしまった" [Grandmother, who was sick, ended up sitting down on the bed] (Sato, 1995, p. 5). In studying the miscue patterns of Japanese readers for the particle は, Ferguson et al. found that Japanese readers did not confuse the two pronunciations of は (ha and wa) when it served as a subject marker. Instead, they tended to substitute は (ha) with another subject marker, が (ga), two phonetically and visually different particles. In sum, these examples underscore the need to delineate reading as a process of meaning construction, as readers draw from language cueing systems and reading strategies to disambiguate written language as they make sense of text.

What the Miscues of Bilingual Readers Tell Us About Reading

Working on the premise that reading is a unified meaning-making and language process, miscue analysis is a way to study the miscues of bilingual readers reading linguistically diverse texts. Miscue analysis was further developed into a set of procedures termed the *Reading Miscue Inventory* (RMI) and includes a set of questions and procedures for conducting varying forms of miscue analysis (Goodman et al., 2005). Appendix A provides a more detailed discussion of the classroom procedure, one of three miscue analysis procedures, used for the Profiles.

Miscue analysis has been used to study the miscue patterns and reading behaviors of bilingual Spanish and English readers (Croce, 2010; Kabuto, 2017, 2018; Miramontes, 1990). One of the significant findings from this body of work contends that oral reading performances in English do not necessarily equate with reading comprehension (Miramontes, 1990; Croce,

2010; Kabuto, 2017; Kim, 2012; Wang, 2021). In other words, comprehension is much more complex for bilingual readers than accurate and automatic word recognition because they are drawing from a diverse set of linguistic resources to make sense of texts, and their reading performance in English did not predict how well bilingual readers understood the text written in another language.

Similar to this chapter, other researchers have used miscue analysis with texts written in other languages and writing systems (Ebe, 2008; Goodman et al., 2012). Romatowski (1981), studying bilingual readers reading texts written in Polish, and Barrera (1981), studying bilingual readers reading Spanish texts, contributed to the earliest studies that used miscue analysis with texts written in another language. Both studies found that there are nonlinear, complex relationships between oral reading miscues and comprehension; readers with a high number of miscues did not always have low comprehension scores.

Ferguson et al. (2012), Kabuto (2005), Kim (2012), and Wang and Gilles (2017) used miscue analysis with Japanese and Chinese texts. Ferguson et al. (2012) and Kim (2012) described the miscue patterns of Japanese readers to show the complexity readers must navigate in spelling and grammatical patterns in Japanese text. In my early work with Emma learning to read Japanese, I found that reading directionality did not impact how she inferred, predicted, and confirmed based on language cueing systems.

Using error analysis, Xu (2012) argued that effective and efficient reading is not dependent on accurately recognizing words. Wang and Gilles (2017) studied Chinese-speaking readers reading Chinese and English texts and found that readers were cognizant of the differences between the two writing systems. They also found that readers did not use the linguistic cueing systems equally across both types of texts, and this impacted their perceptions of themselves as readers.

Observations of Readers

The aforementioned body of research on the miscues of bilingual readers affords a foundation upon which to observe bilingual readers for the Profiles. Observing readers aims to look across bilingual reading behaviors to consider the flexible ways that readers transact with texts when language borders are permeable. The section is built from three sources – the classroom procedure for miscue analysis based on oral readings, oral retellings, and the reflective and collaborative conversations about the readers' high-quality miscues. These sources are elaborated individually in Appendix A.

The oral readings, retellings, and collaborative conversations were conducted with diverse reading materials and in a fluid language context determined by the individuals and materials within that context. Each of these sources of information was triangulated in a way to consider the effectiveness of how the readers used meaning-based strategies to read and comprehend.

Sophie: Observations of a Reader

When I first met Sophie, she said that she believed herself to be a good reader and, in our discussions of reading, she indicated that she felt more comfortable reading English texts. She said, "I like English books. I know how to read Greek, but I don't want to read Greek books." When I asked why, she responded, "I like English." Sophie often talked about the different purposes of speaking, reading, writing, and listening in Greek and English served in her life. Living in a Greek community and communicating with her family in Greece, Sophie articulated that she needed to be able to speak and listen and understand Greek, but she did not express the same need to read and write Greek. In fact, Sophie described the importance of being able to understand Greek as an oral language because she enjoyed listening to stories read to her by her grandmother living in Greece.

Sophie explained her focus on word-solving strategies when she came to something when reading that she did not know. She said that she is "good with the words" and that "I look at them and, without reading, I read them." Sophie said that if she comes to words that she does not know, she will "try to sound it out" or "ask someone for help on how to pronounce" the word.

During our 10-week sessions, Sophie read five books: *The Garden of Abdul Gasazi* (Van Allsburg, 1979), *Yo, Vikings* (Schachner, 2002), Ο Ποντικός της Εξοχής και ο ποντικός της Πόλης [*The Mouse of the Countryside and the City Mouse*] (Aesop, 1995), Ο λαγός και οι Φίλοι του [*The Hare and His Friends*] (Aesop, 1995), and Το καλύτερο σκιουράκι του δάσους [*The Best Squirrel in the Forest*] (Korla, 1975). For ease of discussion, I will use the translated titles for the Greek books. Sophie also read one chapter, Chapter 2, in the book *The Invention of Hugo Cabret* (Selznick, 2007). Documentation of her miscues and retelling patterns suggest that Sophie had a broader range of effective reading and meaning-making strategies when reading both English and Greek texts than she articulated, especially when her reading was placed within a context that allowed for language fluidity.

Sophie's Uses of Language Cueing Systems

Sophie had a high percentage of sentences that were grammatically acceptable across all six books. Table 3.2 shows the percentages that resulted from the miscue analysis and retelling rubrics (see Appendix for how these percentages are calculated). The percentages ranged from 100% syntactic, or grammatical, acceptability (*The Hare and His Friends* and *The Best Squirrel in the Forest*) to 88% grammatical acceptability (*The Mouse of the Countryside and the City Mouse*). When reading *The Garden of Abdul Gasazi*, 97% of the sentences were grammatically acceptable, and for Chapter 2 of *The Invention of Hugo Cabret*, 83% of Sophie's sentences were grammatically acceptable.

Examples of how Sophie used the grammatical cueing system occurred across the Greek and English texts. For instance, Sophie read the sentence,

Table 3.2 Miscue Analysis and Retelling Data for Sophie

Books	*Syntactic Acceptability*	*Semantic Acceptability*	*Meaning Change*	*Graphic Similarity*	*Retelling Score*
English Books					
The Garden of Abdul Gasazi	Yes: 97%	Yes: 95%	No: 100% Yes: 0%	High: 42% Some: 14% None: 42%	3.6
The Invention of Hugo Cabret: Chapter 2	Yes: 83 %	Yes: 83%	No: 100% Yes: 0%	High: 62% Some: 7% None: 15%	3.0
Yo, Vikings	Yes: 96%	Yes: 92%	No: 100% Yes: 0%	High: 40% Some: 30% None: 30%	4.0
Greek Books					
The Mouse of the Countryside and the City Mouse	Yes: 88%	Yes: 75%	No: 92% Yes: 8%	High: 100% Some: 0% None: 0%	3.5
The Hare and His Friends	Yes: 100%	Yes: 92%	No: 100% Yes: 0%	High: 50% Some: 50% None: 0%	3.5
The Best Squirrel in the Forest	Yes: 100%	Yes: 87%	No: 97% Yes: 3%	High: 80% Some: 20% None: 0%	4.0

"When Alan took the bird in his arms, ***it*** tried to give him a bite" (Van Allsburg, 1979, p. 11) as "When Alan took the bird in his arms, ***he*** tried to give him a bite." Sophie self-corrected the substitution. Communicating the nuanced meaning of pronouns within the sentence, Sophie explained that she self-corrected, "Because *he* kind of sounds like it's Allen trying to give him a bite. Usually with animals you say *it*."

When reading *The Best Squirrel in the Forest*, Sophie read the sentence, "Η καρίδα χτίπισε τα κοτοπουλιάκια **στα κεφαλάκια** . . ." [The walnut hit the chicks on their heads . . .] (Korla, 1975, p. 9) as "Η καρίδα χτίπισε τα κοτοπουλιάκια **κεφάλη** . . ." [The walnut hit the chicks on their head . . .]. Sophie self-corrected to the expected response because having the singular and plural forms of the noun *head* made a difference in the sentence. She said, "There were a lot of κοτοπουλάκια [chicks] and κεφάλη [head] means only one. So κεφαλάκια [heads] would (refer to) all the chicks."

The semantic acceptability across the six books ranged from 95% (*The Garden of Abdul Gasazi*) to 75% (*The Mouse of the Countryside and the City Mouse*). When considered together, Sophie read *The Garden of Abdul Gasazi*, *Yo, Vikings*, and *The Hare and His Friends* with the highest semantic acceptability. The lowest semantic acceptability occurred when reading *The Mouse of the Countryside and the City Mouse* and Chapter 2 of the *Invention of Hugo Cabret.*

Semantic acceptability is considered in tandem with grammatical acceptability because if a sentence is not grammatically acceptable, it will not make sense (Goodman et al., 2005). Previously, I described how Sophie self-corrected κεφάλη [head] to κεφαλάκια [heads] because she needed the plural form of the noun. Reading the word in its singular form was not only grammatically unacceptable but it also did not make sense to her. Sophie presented a similar self-correction pattern when reading *The Garden of Abdul Gasazi*. She read the sentence, "You see, Alan, no one can really turn dogs into ducks; that old magician just made you think that the ***duck*** was Fritz" (Van Allsburg, 1979, p. 13) as "You see, Alan, no one can really turn dogs into ducks; that old magician just made you think that the ***ducks*** was Fritz" and self-corrected to *duck*. Reading the plural form of the word *duck* disrupted the grammatical structure of the sentence and, hence, the meaning.

In another example in which grammar and meaning were balanced, Sophie read the sentence from *The Garden of Abdul Gasazi* (Van Allsburg, 1979, p. 11), "Running along with one arm, reaching for the hat, Alan lost his hold ***on*** Fritz" as "Running along with one arm, reaching for the hat, Alan lost his hold ***of*** Fritz." Sophie's high-quality substitution maintained the grammar of the sentence and resulted in a meaningful sentence.

Sophie also used the semantic cueing system to self-correct mispronunciations of words. For instance, Sophie read the sentence from *The Mouse of the Countryside and the City Mouse*, "Τι ***πλούσιο*** φαγοπότι ¨ φώναξε κατάπληκτος ο ποντικός της εξοχής όταν είδε το τραπέζι στρωμένο" ["What fine dining," yelled the wonderstruck city mouse when he saw the table set] (Aesop, 1995, p. 4) as "Τι ***πλόσιο*** φαγοπότι ¨ φώναξε κατάπληκτος ο ποντικός της εξοχής όταν είδε το τραπέζι στρωμένο." She mispronounced *πλούσιο* ("fine" as in "fine dining") as /πλόσιο/ and self-corrected to the expected word. When asked why she self-corrected, Sophie responded, "Because if you say /πλόσιο/, it doesn't make sense, so I corrected to πλούσιο." When probed a little further into why she self-corrected, Sophie referred to the graphic cueing system to say, "When I was reading and made the miscue, I went back and saw that it was another (word). I saw it was πλου (pointing to the letters in the word)."

Sophie's miscue patterns and reflections illustrate how she attended to the graphophonic information in the text and, more importantly, balanced that information with the syntactic and semantic cueing systems. The graphic similarity of the word-for-word substitutions varied across the texts, with the greatest variance occurring in the English texts. For instance, when reading *The Garden of Abdul Gasazi*, Sophie made a total of 13 word substitutions, and 42% of them were high in graphic similarity. She read *bitten* as *bitter* and *duck* and as *ducks*. At the same time, 42% of the word substitutions had no graphic similarity. When reading Greek texts, Sophie tended to depend more heavily on the graphophonic cueing system, as illustrated by *The Mouse of the Countryside and the City Mouse*. Sophie made 15-word substitutions, and 100% of those were high in graphic similarity.

Reading Comprehension

Sophie provided effective retellings across all the texts she read. The holistic retellings scores ranged from 3 to 4 (Table 3.2). She received a holistic retelling score of 3 for her retelling of Chapter 2 of *The Invention of Hugo Cabret.* She was able to give an overall description of the chapter but had difficulty with some details in the chapter. *The Invention of Hugo Cabret* differs from the other texts because it was a chapter from a book. As such, Sophie was in the process of building knowledge of the story characters and setting. Book chapters are generally difficult to use in determining a reader's overall understanding because the storyline may be fragmented from the rest of the book (Goodman et al., 2005).

When Sophie read *The Best Squirrel in the Forest,* she received a holistic retelling score of 4 and a retelling score of 3.5 when she read the other two Greek books. After Sophie read *The Mouse of the Countryside and the City Mouse,* Despina said in Greek, "Now, this story that you read, what was it about?" This prompted Sophie to retell the story in Greek as follows:

> About two mice that went to visit their homes. The city mouse went to see his cousin, the country mouse.

With follow-up questions, Sophie presented more details in Greek as follows:

- The country mouse left when he heard how beautiful his cousin's house was.
- He has wine, desserts, cheese, and fruit.
- They went to the city mouse's hideout (when the cat came).

After the aided retelling in Greek, Sophie then seamlessly summarized the retelling in English:

> So when the mouse of the city goes to visit his cousin, he likes the house. But when his cousin goes to see his house, he's amazed. And when they're eating, a cat comes and chases them. And when they go into the mouse of the city's hiding spot, the mouse of the country left and he went and missed his house a lot.

A Summary of Sophie's Bilingual Reading Behaviors

Observations and documentation of Sophie's bilingual reading behaviors offer a more complicated picture of Sophie than she described at the beginning of our sessions. In our opening interview, Sophie said that when she was having difficulty with reading, she would "try to sound it out" or "ask someone for help on how to pronounce" the word. This word-oriented view was further supported by Sophie's comment describing herself as "good with the words" because, as she explained, "I look at them and, without reading, I read them."

Analyzing Sophie's oral reading and entering into collaborative discussions with her, however, suggested that reading was more than reading the words. Rather, she was cognizant of the diverse ways that she approached reading and why she made miscues. Regardless of the written language of the text, Sophie balanced the three cueing systems to read for meaning. Having a meaning-centered approach to reading was also evidenced in her retellings. Sophie exhibited a self-awareness of her bilingual reading behaviors. Through collaborative discussions, she developed a way to talk about why she made miscues that did not necessarily draw from reading behaviors like "sounding out words," "reading too fast," or "asking for assistance."

Mai: Observations of a Reader

Mai was a Japanese- and English-speaking second-grade student attending a public school with English-only curricular instruction. Mai was born in Tokyo, Japan, and her family moved to the United States when she was 4 years old. She received English as a New Language (ENL) services five days a week and attended a Japanese heritage school on Saturdays.

Mai expressed that she was more comfortable speaking, reading, and writing in Japanese. Because her family was in the United States for only a short amount of time (up to five years), Mai was expected to return to Japan and assimilate back into Japanese schooling. As such, she attended a Japanese heritage language school on Saturdays where she studied Japanese history, math, and language arts.

I met with Mai in four sessions, and she read three books for her Profile: the short stories *Spring* and *The Story* from The Frog and Toad series (Lobel, 2011), *Straw Maid* (Lobel, 1983), and あひる の たまご [*The Duck's Egg*] (Sato, 1995). When asked what she does when she has difficulties with reading, Mai responded that she "sounds it out" or "asks for help." She did not articulate other strategies. Observations and documentation of Mai's bilingual reading behaviors suggest that Mai had more diverse reading and meaning strategies than she described, but these strategies were not consistent across the English and Japanese texts. She exhibited a broader range of effective reading behaviors when she read *The Duck's Egg*. When reading the short stories from the Frog and Toad series and *Straw Maid*, Mai tended to pay significant attention to the graphophonic information in the written text. As a result, she produced miscues that resulted in meaning loss. Table 3.3 outlines the percentages from the miscue analysis and retellings.

Mai's Uses of Language Cueing Systems

Mai read with a higher percentage of grammatically acceptable sentences when reading the Japanese text *The Duck's Egg*; 91% of the total number of sentences were grammatically acceptable. She demonstrated flexibility in reading verb forms and provided a number of high-quality miscues that did

Table 3.3 Miscue Analysis and Retelling Data for Mai

Books	*Syntactic Acceptability*	*Semantic Acceptability*	*Meaning Change*	*Graphic Similarity*	*Retelling Score*
English Books					
Spring	Yes: 79%	Yes: 59%	No: 100% Yes: 0%	High: 81% Some: 13% None: 6%	*2.3/3.5
The Story	Yes: 77%	Yes: 75%	No: 100% Yes: 0%	High: 94% Some: 6% None: 0%	*2.0/4
Straw Maid	Yes: 81%	Yes: 61%	No: 98% Yes: 2%	High: 72% Some: 20% None: 8%	2.0
Japanese Books					
The Duck's Egg	Yes: 91%	Yes: 89%	No: 100% Yes: 0%	High: 100% Some: 0% None: 0%	3.5

* *Mai retold Spring and The Story from the Frog and Toad series in English and then in Japanese. Mai's retelling scores of 2.3 and 2.0 reflect the English retelling, and her scores of 3.5 and 4 reflect the Japanese retelling.*

not impact the grammatical structure of the sentences. In Japanese, not only do verbs occur in the past and present tense, they can also be represented in a formal or informal form. These forms do not change the meaning or the grammar of the sentence. For instance, Mai read the sentence, "あひるが たまごを あたためだすと、 すぐに ひよこが **うまれた**" [As soon as Duck warmed the egg, Chick was born] (Sato, 1995, p. 25) with the formal form of the verb まれました. Both forms have the same meaning "was born," and the difference in the two forms represents a formality.

Similarly, Mai made other types of complex verb form substitutions. In Japanese, the endings of verbs can change to indicate not just a form change, but also a change in emphasis on the action of the verb. Mai read the sentence, "へ やへ はいった ばばばあちゃんは、 すぐに べっどに **すわりこんでしまった**" [Grandmother, who was sick, ended up sitting down on the bed] (Sato, 1995, p. 5) as "へ やへ はいった ばばばあちゃんは、 すぐに べっどに **すわりこみました**" [Grandmother, who was sick, immediately sat down on the bed]. The two verb phrases have similar meanings, and Mai's substitution placed more immediacy on sitting down on the bed than the written text.

When reading *Spring*, *The Story*, and *Straw Maid*, however, Mai produced sentences that had lower grammatical acceptability when compared to reading the Japanese book. For *Spring*, 79% of the total number of sentences Mai read were grammatically acceptable, and for *Straw Maid*, 81% were grammatically acceptable. As an example, Mai read the sentence from *Spring*, "And it ***means*** that we can begin a whole new year together, Toad" (Lobel, 2011,

p. 8) as "And it ***must*** that we can begin a whole new year, Toad." Mai substituted ***must*** for ***means*** and omitted the word ***together***. While the omission of ***together*** did not disrupt the grammatical structure of the sentence, the substitution of ***must*** for ***means*** resulted in a sentence that was not grammatically correct.

There were times, however, when Mai effectively used the grammatical cueing system. When reading *The Story*, she read the sentence, "'***Why are*** you banging your head against the wall?' asked Frog" (Lobel, 2011, p. 24) as "'***Were*** you banging your head against the wall?' asked Frog." When asked why she thought she read the sentence as "'Were you banging your head against the wall?' asked Frog," Mai replied, "I saw an 'e' at the end of 'are' so I wasn't sure how to pronounce the word. *E*, *i*, and *y* are confusing to me, and I sometimes don't know how to say the word." This is an example of an elected miscue in which Mai purposely made a miscue in order to maintain the grammar and meaning of the sentence. She said that her complex miscue made sense so she did not need to correct it.

Overall, however, Mai was not as successful in producing meaningful sentences when reading *Spring*, *The Story*, and *Straw Maid* because she sometimes relied too much on the graphophonic cueing system to produce words that were visually similar to the target word but did not always make sense. In *Spring*, 79% of the total sentences Mai read made sense, and in *Straw Maid*, 61% were meaningful. The main indication of Mai's overreliance on the graphophonic cueing system was the number of word substitutions that were high in graphic similarity and nonword substitutions. In fact, when reading *Spring*, the majority of Mai's miscues were substitutions (51 of 57 total miscues). For instance, Mai read *page* as /pag/ in the sentence, "Frog tore off the November page" (Lobel, 2011, p. 12). Of the 57 miscues, Mai self-corrected eight.

Throughout our conversations about her miscues, Mai regularly referred to the graphophonic cueing system, even if she produced sentences that had meaning. For instance, she read the sentence, "They put the girl in ***a*** sack" (Lobel, 1983, p. 16) as "They put the girl in ***the*** sack." When I inquired into the miscue, she explained that the miscue "did not make sense" because the word is *a* and not *the*. She also said that she should have corrected the miscue. Mai's interpretation of her miscue was based on what was visually present in the text, rather than what made sense in a meaning-centered way.

Mai did not show the same dependence on the graphic information when reading *The Duck's Egg*. When reading this book, 89% of the total sentences that Mai read made sense. In addition, she made 18 miscues and, of 18, 12 were word substitutions. Seventy-five percent of the substitutions were high in graphic similarity. These observations suggest that Mai balanced and flexibly used the graphophonic information with the other two cueing systems.

As a result, she made more high-quality miscues and self-corrections and rarely made nonword substitutions. For instance, Mai read the sentence "**あるひ**、ばばばあちやん が、おなかを かかえて かえってきたの をめて、 こいぬと こねこは いった" [One day, Dog and Cat said that the grandmother came back with a stomach ache] (Sato, 1995, p. 3). She started the sentence with あひ [ahi] because she most likely thought the word would read あひる [duck] instead of あるひ [one day]. The two words share three hiragana forms, but two of them had switched places. When asked why she self-corrected, Mai said that あひる [duck] would not make sense with the rest of the sentence, so she needed to self-correct to あるひ [one day].

Reading Comprehension

Mai's retelling scores varied not only by the language of the text but also by how she was able to use languages within a translanguaging context. Based on the holistic retelling rubric, Mai appeared to have the lowest retelling scores when reading *Spring* and *The Story* (scores of 2.3 and 2.0, respectively) and the *Straw Maid* (a score of 2). These scores, however, were more reflective of Mai's ability to express her understanding of the story when the retelling was limited to English.

Mai's miscue statistics for grammatical and semantic acceptability for *The Story* were 77% and 75%, respectively. Therefore, roughly 25% of all the sentences were not grammatically acceptable and did not make sense. When I asked Mai to retell *The Story* in English, she did not provide a detailed retelling, and it was difficult to follow because she used the pronoun *he* rather than the names of the characters. Mai's retelling is as follows:

> Frog was first sick. He said tell me a story. He think and he think but he not think. But his head is hurting so he trade with Frog and he told a story and he sleeping and he got something.

Noticing the lack of details and the difficulty Mai had in using English to retell the story, I asked her to retell the story in Japanese. She received a score of 4.0 for her Japanese retelling, which follows:

> At first, Frog was sick. Toad brought tea for Frog. An then Frog asked if Toad would tell him a story. He kept thinking of a story. And he did things like hit his head, turn upside down, pour water on his head. Then his head began to hurt and he went to bed and he traded. Frog was feeling better so he traded with Toad, and he told a story. Because any story was okay, he told a story about what Toad did earlier. When the story was over Toad had fallen asleep. So he left to go somewhere.

Mai's Japanese retelling of *The Story* was not only more cohesive and easier to follow but also the retelling provided more details and incorporated story language and actions. For instance, Mai noted that Toad poured water on himself to think of a story. Mai was also able to better articulate the problem in the story and the story conclusion. Mai's retelling in English does not demonstrate the depth of her understanding of the story. By drawing on

Japanese, she could demonstrate her competence as a reader who understood the story regardless of her miscue percentages.

Mai's retelling of *The Duck's Egg* was detailed and contained vocabulary and phrases from the story. Part of her retelling in Japanese is as follows:

> The grandmother went to look for the eggs, but she went back to bed. Everyone was worried. They thought that the grandmother was sick. They gathered fruits and vegetables for the grandmother. And then the duck knocked on the door and asked everyone if they knew where her eggs went. Grandmother heated up the eggs and everyone knew that she wasn't really sick. Everyone wondered what they should do with all the food, and they decided to have a birthday party for the chicks.

A Summary of Mai's Bilingual Reading Behaviors

There is evidence of Mai balancing the three cueing systems to read for meaning. At the same time, she approached reading and problem solving slightly differently with the texts. When reading stories from the *Frog and Toad* series and *Straw Maid*, she depended on the graphophonic cueing system and did not always balance this cueing system with meaning. As a result, she produced nonwords or word substitutions that did not always make sense in the sentences. Her effective problem solving, however, surfaced when she read *The Duck's Egg*. Mai balanced the three cueing systems to take a meaning-centered approach to reading.

At the same time, Mai's ability to communicate her comprehension was the direct result of the language fluidity in the reading context. The syntactic and semantic acceptability percentages did little to indicate the level of her understanding of *Spring* and *The Story*. As Mai's Profile illustrated, using a bilingual reader's oral reading performance to predict their comprehension is misleading and cannot be determined by a number.

Lessons Learned From the Profiles

Sophie's and Mai's bilingual reading behaviors, as observed and documented through their miscues, retellings, and reflective conversations, are quite revelatory of the complex and inconsistent relationships among language, reading, and comprehension. In line with other research (e.g., González, 2012; Sanchez et al., 2013; Ascenzi-Moreno, 2018), dominant reading assessment practices that require the sole use of English disenfranchise bilingual readers who exhibit complex reading behaviors when reading across different writing systems. Both Japanese and Greek have little commonalities with the English writing system, and yet, Mai and Sophie had little difficulty moving across languages when reading and retelling stories.

Returning to aspects of their learning biographies, Mai and Sophie, interestingly, indicated that they used the "sounding out strategy" when it came to words they did not know. Sophie's bilingual reading behaviors illustrate that she seldom used this strategy. Mai, on the other hand, exhibited behaviors that showed reliance on the graphophonic information when she read *Spring* and *Straw Maid*, but not when reading the Japanese book. It is highly likely that their use of the term was more associated with an English-dominant view of reading and reflects a social model of reading defined by a discourse on what "good readers" do (Gee, 2002; Compton-Lilly, 2005). By stating that they sound out words, Mai and Sophie aligned themselves with the dominant discourse in the classroom and a school-based model of reading. Their Profiles show the importance of not accepting taken-for-granted discourses like "sounding out" but rather using close observations of what readers actually do when they are engaged with texts to document their bilingual reading behaviors.

Supported by other studies, Sophie's and Mai's oral reading behaviors and performances were not indicators of what they knew about the story and how they were able to communicate that meaning. Sophie's miscue statistics showed that there was more variability in her oral readings than in her retelling scores across all the texts. Her retellings of the Greek stories also presented differences, depending on whether she retold in English or Greek. The Greek retelling of *The Mouse of the Countryside and the City Mouse* tended to be brief and, with the aided retelling, she provided more details that came directly from the story. Her retelling in English, however, was concise, presenting an overview of the story from start to finish. Each retelling captured different aspects of Sophie's comprehension. By only looking at the Greek retelling, we might erroneously assume that Sophie could not provide a story summary and needed probing for the details. By only considering the English retelling, we might conversely and mistakenly assume that Sophie was unable to articulate the details of the story. Without considering language as a unified system of meaning-making, we would miss the landscape of performance styles and ways that Sophie was able to demonstrate her understanding.

Mai's Profile suggest a similar, but different, situation when she read and retold *The Story*. Mai's English retelling of *The Story* did little to represent her understanding of the story. As her Profile suggests, her retelling in English was vague with few details. Her retelling of *The Story* in Japanese, however, presented a different picture. She provided a chronological and linear retelling with details taken straight from the story. Without balancing the retelling in English with that done in Japanese, Mai's oral reading and comprehension could have been misinterpreted, measured by the language of the written text rather than the deep meaning that the reader constructed. Clearly, Mai was able to understand the text in spite of having miscue percentages on the lower end when reading all three books. Mai's and Sophie's Profiles exemplify that comprehending text and communicating that understanding in a particular context are multidimensional and draw from an array of social, linguistic, cognitive, and semiotic factors.

The next chapter will take a closer look into the translanguaging context to explore bilingual reading behaviors through a discussion of code-switching research. The considerable body of research on code-switching supplements our understanding of how the translanguaging context was co-constructed among participants and mediated by books by providing a model for language-in-use. In Chapter 4, I will provide a contemporary twist to the concept of code-switching to explore how the strategic movement among linguistic forms that construct a dynamic translanguaging context supports bilingual readers.

References

Aesop. (1995). *The hare and his friends*. Angyra.

Aesop. (1995). *The mouse of the countryside and the city mouse*. Recos.

Ascenzi-Moreno, L. (2018). Translanguaging and responsive assessment adaptations: Emergent bilingual readers through the lens of possibility. *Language Arts*, *95*(6), 355–368.

Barrera, R. (1981). Reading in Spanish: Insights from children's miscues. In S. Hudelson (Ed.), *Learning to read in different languages* (pp. 1–9). Linguistic and Literacy Series: Papers in Applied Linguistics. Center for Applied Linguistics.

Compton-Lilly, C. (2005). "Sounding out": A pervasive cultural model of reading. *Language Arts*, *82*(6), 441–451.

Croce, K. A. (2010). Exploring assessment of students from different language backgrounds: A look at reading comprehension using informational texts. *English in Education*, *44*(2), 125–145.

Ebe, A. (2008). What eye movement and miscue analysis reveals about the reading process of young bilinguals. In A. D. Flurkey, E. J. Paulson, & K. S. Goodman (Eds.), *Scientific realism in studies of reading* (pp. 131–149). Lawrence Erlbaum.

Ferguson, D., Kato, Y., & Nagahiro, M. (2012). Miscues and eye movements of Japanese beginner readers. In K. Goodman, S. Wang, M. Iventosch, & Y. Goodman (Eds.), *Reading in Asian languages: Making sense of written texts in Chinese, Japanese, and Korean* (pp. 127–143). Routledge.

Garcia, O., & Wei, L. (2014). *Translanguaging: Language, bilingualism, and education*. Palgrave MacMillan.

Gee, J. (2002). A sociocultural perspective on early literacy development. In S. Neuman & D. Dickinson (Eds.), *Handbook of early literacy research* (pp. 30–42). Guilford Press.

González, V. (2012). Assessment of bilingual/multilingual pre-K-Grade 12 students: A critical discussion of past, present, and future issues. *Theory into Practice*, *51*, 290–296.

Goodman, K. (1996). *On reading*. Heinemann.

Goodman, K. (2011). The process of reading in non-alphabetic languages. In K. Goodman, S. Wang, M. Iventosch, & Y. Goodman (Eds.), *Reading in Asian languages: Making sense of written texts in Chinese, Japanese, and Korean* (pp. 3–15). Routledge.

Goodman, K., Wang, S., Iventosch, M., & Goodman, Y. M. (Eds.). (2012). *Reading in Asian languages: Making sense of written texts in Chinese, Japanese, and Korean*. Routledge.

Goodman, Y., Watson, D., & Burke, C. L. (2005). *Reading miscue inventory: From evaluation to instruction* (2nd ed.). Richard C. Owen.

Kabuto, B. (2005). Understanding early biliteracy development through book-handling behaviors. *Talking Points*, *16*(2), 10–15.

Kabuto, B. (2014). A semiotic perspective on reading picture books: The case of *Alexander and the Wind-Up Mouse. Linguistics and Education, 25*(1), 12–24.

Kabuto, B. (2015). The construction of biliterate narratives and identities between parents and children. *Global Education Review, 2*(2), 7–23.

Kabuto, B. (2017). A socio-psycholinguistic perspective on biliteracy: The use of miscue analysis as a culturally relevant assessment tool. *Reading Horizons, 56*(1), 25–44.

Kabuto, B. (2018). Becoming a bilingual reader as linguistic and identity enactments. *Talking Points, 29*(2), 11–18.

Kado, K. (2017). Learning to read Japanese. In L. Verhoeven & C. Perfetti (Eds.), *Learning to read across languages and writing systems* (pp. 57–81). Cambridge University Press.

Kim, K. (2012). How readers process Japanese orthography in two different texts. In K. Goodman, S. Wang, M. Iventosch, & Y. Goodman (Eds.), *Reading in Asian languages: Making sense of written texts in Chinese, Japanese, and Korean* (pp. 144–157). Routledge.

Korla. (1975). *The best squirrel in the forest.* Angyra.

Lobel, A. (1983). *Straw maid.* Greenwillow Books.

Lobel, A. (2011). Spring. In *Frog and toad are friends* (pp. 4–15). Harper Collins.

Lobel, A. (2011). The Story. In *Frog and toad are friends* (pp. 16–27). Harper Collins.

Miramontes, O. (1990). Comparative study of English oral reading skills in differently schooled groups of Hispanic students. *Journal of Literacy Research, 22*(4), 373–394.

Rogers, H. (2005). *Writing systems: A linguistic approach.* Blackwell Publishing.

Romatowski, J. (1981). A study of oral reading in Polish and English: A psycholinguistic perspective. In S. Hudelson (Ed.), *Learning to reading in different languages* (pp. 21–26). Linguistic and Literacy Series: Papers in Applied Linguistics. Center for Applied Linguistics.

Sanchez, S. V., Rodriguez, B. J., Soto-Huerta, M. E., Villarreal, F. C., Guerra, N. S., & Flores, B. B. (2013). A case for multidimensional bilingual assessment. *Language Assessment Quarterly, 10*(2), 160–177.

Sato, W. (1995). *Ahiru no Tamago.* Fukuinkan-Shoten.

Schachner, J. B. (2002). *Yo, Vikings!* Dutton Children's Books.

Selznick, B. (2007). *The invention of Hugo Cabret.* Scholastic.

Van Allsburg, C. (1979). *The garden of Abdul Gasazi.* HMH Books for Young Readers.

Verhoeven, L. T. W., & Perfetti, C. A. (2017). Introduction: Operating principles in learning to read. In L. Verhoeven & C. Perfetti (Eds.), *Learning to read across languages and writing systems* (pp. 1–30). Cambridge University Press.

Wang, Y. (2021). Adult English learners and the bilingual reading process: Retrospective miscue analysis. *Bilingual Research Journal*, 433–449.

Wang, Y., & Gilles, C. J. (2017). Reading in English and in Chinese: Case study of retrospective miscue analysis with two adult ELLs. *Reading Horizons, 56*(2), 64–92.

Xu, J. (2012). Making sense in reading Chinese: An error-detection study. In K. Goodman, S. Wang, M. Iventosch, & Y. Goodman (Eds.), *Reading in Asian languages: Making sense of written texts in Chinese, Japanese, and Korean* (pp. 158–190). Routledge.

4 Profiles of Code-Switching in a Translanguaging Context

While translanguaging has taken a commanding lead in reframing linguistically diverse language behaviors as fluid, transformative, and deeply connected to practice, it has also developed a complicated relationship with the well-studied concept of code-switching (Cummins, 2017; Otheguy et al., 2019; MacSwan, 2017). Some translanguaging scholars reject the notion of code-switching because they argue that it originates from a theoretical frame of languages as autonomous entities that are broken down into codes (Otheguy et al., 2019). The long-accepted definition of code-switching has, in fact, described it as the use of speech that includes languages from two distinct grammatical systems, first and second languages, within the same exchange (Gumperz, 1982). For many translanguaging scholars, differentiating translanguaging, as the "linguistics of participation," from code-switching, as the "linguistics of systems," was the key to exploring how language use, particularly in classrooms, formed new language practices that led to the construction of knowledge that goes beyond the structure of language in and of itself (Wei & Lin, 2019).

In this chapter, I redefine code-switching as moving among a range of available linguistic forms and resources to take a closer look at code-switching through Emma's and Jenny's Profiles. Code-switching is not limited to switching between languages as named language systems or language codes nor is it interchangeable with the term translanguaging. Linguistic resources can range from morphological to syntactic to socio-psycholinguistic to semiotic knowledge and represent the full range of meaning-making tools in linguistically diverse students' linguistic repertoires (Otheguy et al., 2019).

Research on code-switching, however, has provided invaluable insights into challenging this language behavior as deficit-oriented alterations representative of linguistic incompetence (Yow et al., 2018). In fact, code-switching researchers argue that bilingual speakers systematically resource language forms in functional and meaningful ways that can uncover speakers' sophisticated knowledge of grammar (Yow et al., 2018). Linguistic forms have histories (Rogers, 2005) and, as Cummins (2017) argued, they "exist in the lives and experiences of teachers, students, government, politicians, and countless agencies, and they generate an immense material and

DOI: 10.4324/9781003045984-5

symbolic reality" (p. 11). As such, the movement and negotiation of language forms assist in studying the development of socially constructed roles and responsibilities within social practices that contest or reproduce ideologies of language and social and cultural identities. As a result, there has been an attempt to marry frameworks on translanguaging with those of code-switching. Karlsson (2016) and Yow et al. (2018), for instance, contend that associating code-switching with linguistic competence is not much different from viewing translanguaging as a language practice built upon linguistic resources for the sake of any sense-making process in the classroom, families, and communities.

My interest in integrating a code-switching lens centers on conceptualizing a model of language-in-use to examine how bilingual readers negotiate linguistic forms and meaning in reading events as they transact with text. Researchers have engaged in similar endeavors (Cahyani et al., 2018) to suggest that code-switching functions can inform our understanding of translanguaging as part of bilingual repertoires and practices. For me, code-switching holds a particular relevance to understanding what happens when multiple language forms come together to produce a blending of not only literacy practices but also language as a semiotic system so that language forms are considered modal resources (Wei & Lin, 2019). As seen in Chapter 3, reading events involve both oral language and written text, both of which are composed of different forms. Bilingual readers negotiate these forms in order to construct and be able to communicate the deep meaning they create with texts.

In this chapter, I will take considerable liberty in merging a translanguaging perspective with code-switching to illustrate how code-switching provides a means for slowing down the conversational moves to discuss the ways in which bilingual forms are proposed, taken up, or even rejected in bilingual reading events. Through this framework, language is not additive but negotiated through natural, in-the-moment interactions around texts. This process of the doing of language is, I argue, critical to the construction of a translanguaging context.

My approach falls in line with a growing number of researchers calling for inclusive perspectives on translanguaging and code-switching (e.g., Karlsson, 2016; Poza, 2017). MacSwan (2017), for instance, argues that the large body of research on code-switching from sociolinguistic perspectives to bilingualism challenges deficit orientations of bilingualism to suggest that "codeswitching may be seen as an instance of translanguaging, alongside other bilingual phenomena such as translation, borrowing, and additional processes, in a range of modalities" (p. 191). Wei (2011) similarly suggested, "For me, translanguaging is both going between different linguistic structures and systems, including different modalities (speaking, writing, signing, listening, reading, remembering) and going beyond them" (p. 2). Code-switching, as the movement among semiotic and linguistic forms, creates unique language patterns that support the reading process and the translanguaging context.

Background on Code-Switching

Code-switching includes switches in forms that occur in any part of a grammatical structure within or across sentence boundaries. For instance, in Chapter 2, I introduced the code-switching interactions among Livia, Maria, and Thomas around Thomas's substitution of *un psicólogo* with *una psicóloga* in the sentence from *Yo, Naomi Leon*, "Naomi fue a *un psicólogo* durante dos años" [Naomi went to a psychologist for two years] (Ryan, 2005, p. 25).

Line 1: Livia said, "Did you hear what you did? What did you do?"
Line 2: Thomas replied, "I said una psicóloga." [a female psychologist]
Line 3: Livia clarified how the text should read, "And what is it?"
Line 4: Thomas replied, "Un psicólogo." [a male psychologist]
Line 5: Livia turned to Maria and said in Spanish, "Thomas said psychologist (feminine form), but its psychologist (masculine form). He did the same thing three times."
Line 6: Livia said to Thomas in English, "Three times, Thomas, you did the same thing."

This excerpt shows two types of switches. Line 2 represents a single word or phrase switch in the sentence, which some researchers have argued is not representative of "true" switches and more reflective of borrowing (Gumperz, 1982). Livia opened the reflective discussion of Thomas's substitution of *un psicólogo* for *una psicóloga* by asking "Did you hear what you did?" Thomas responded, "I said una psicóloga." Disputing the idea of "true" switches, I contend that Thomas's use of *una psicóloga* is a switch because it represents the selection of diverse language forms available in the context. Notwithstanding the argument that the concept of a "word" is difficult to define across the diverse range of languages (Verhoeven & Perfetti, 2017), I argue that Thomas intelligently merged the lexical structures of English and Spanish to generate a meaningful new language practice. Thomas's use of *una psicóloga* reflected his understanding of the text and language. More importantly, acknowledging Thomas's use of *una psicóloga* as a switch also intentionally views language as a constructed process of doing language.

Line 5 represents the second type of switch that occurs across grammatical structures and, in this instance, sentence boundaries. In Line 5, Livia opened the exchange by talking with Maria in Spanish to explain Thomas's miscue. After she said, "He did the same thing three times" in Spanish to Maria, Livia addressed Thomas in English saying, "Three times, Thomas, you did the same thing." Livia's switch represents a second attempt that rephrases what she communicated to Maria, emphasizing the idea that Thomas repeated the miscue three times.

Code-switching has both short- and long-term conversational goals (Heller, 1988). In the previous excerpt, the short-term goal centered on the reflective dialogue around a high-quality miscue so that Thomas would become a metacognitive bilingual reader. In addition, slowing down the interactions to examine the use of language forms underscores how the practice was constructed by participation in the event. In other words, and as we will see with Jenny's Profile later, Livia engaged in *in-the-moment assessment practices* as she evaluated Thomas's responses and responded to Thomas and Maria. Livia strategically included Maria in events by drawing on available forms to allow her to be an active participant.

As part of the long-term goal, Thomas was supported as a bilingual reader, and this support extended across learning contexts. This goal has a temporal nature as well because it can only be reached over time, as these types of events repeat themselves over days, weeks, months, and years (Lemke, 2000). While a translanguaging context accounts for the dynamic use of language in literacy practices, code-switching, as conversational moves, evolves as novice readers move toward becoming independent readers and as participants observe and react to the developing bilingual reading behaviors of readers. Both of these will transform literacy practices and reader identities so that no reading event will look the same, serve the same function, involve the same type of bilingual reading behaviors, and conclude with the same results over time.

The Profiles in this chapter illustrate two important functions of code-switching. Emma's Profile highlights how code-switching served as a problem-solving tool as she worked through the reading process. Jenny's Profile considers a more holistic view of bilingual reading behaviors as readers transform from novice to independent readers. Jenny's code-switching is viewed in two points in time to document the changes in code-switching and how it supported bilingual readers to be competent in a translanguaging context.

Emma: Profile of Code-Switching as a Window Into the Reading Process

Emma was born in Tokyo, Japan, and we have lived in New York since she was 2 years old. Raised in a bilingual household, the fluidity of language use between Japanese and English was the reality more than illusional boundaries of language separation. Although Emma's father and I decided that I would speak English and her father would speak Japanese with her, there was a natural dynamic that was also supported by books, materials, videos, and other items that represented the linguistic diversity of the family. In addition, we enrolled Emma in a Saturday Japanese heritage school, the same school attended by Mai, whom readers met in Chapter 3, in order to support Emma's continued Japanese communication when we moved to New York.

As a bilingual reader, code-switching was uniquely characteristic of reading events that involved texts written in Japanese. This observation speaks to the critical period when Emma was receiving reading instruction in kindergarten and first grade at her local school, whose curriculum was taught in English. As a result, Emma naturally built a preference and dominance for reading texts in English. In fact, I documented that when Emma entered kindergarten, she started working out parts of identity – on the one hand, presenting herself as a bilingual and biliterate child by reading and writing in Japanese in school and, on the other hand, declaring that she did not want to be Japanese anymore. By the time she was in first grade, Emma created dueling but permeable language boundaries so that Japanese connected her to home and family, and English was for school.

Emma's Profile focuses on her oral readings and retellings, when she was 6 years old and in first grade, of three Japanese books: かさ [*Umbrella*] (Matsuno, 1985), うしろにいるのだれ *[Who Is Behind Me?]* (Fukuda, 2004), and おつきさまこんばんは *[Good Evening, Moon]* (Hayashi, 1986). Table 4.1 provides the miscue statistics for her oral reading of the texts and shows the variability in the percentage of sentences that are syntactically and semantically acceptable. Emma read *Who Is Behind Me?* with the highest percentage of grammatically acceptable and meaningful sentences and *Good Evening Moon* with the lowest. Regardless of the miscue percentages, Emma demonstrated a clear understanding of the stories. While I indicated a retelling score, it should be read with caution because early picture books, such as the ones that were part of Emma's Profile, are limited in ascertaining what readers know about detailed story elements like character and plot development, problem and solution, and theme. For instance, Emma retold *Who Is Behind Me?* in English as "It was about these animals and asking what was in front, end, back, and up and down from them" and gave a list of the animals in the story. Because the story itself lacks a comprehensive plot, details, and overall and complete story development, Emma provided an effective retelling, as the story itself was limited in what information she could provide in her retelling.

Pulling back the curtain on miscue statistics gives a closer look into the strategic manner in which Emma resourced linguistic forms as she read. Let us first consider her reading of *Who Is Behind Me?* The book has

Table 4.1 Miscue Analysis and Retelling Data for Emma

Books	*Syntactic Acceptability*	*Semantic Acceptability*	*Meaning Change*	*Graphic Similarity*	*Retelling Score*
Japanese Books					
Umbrella	Yes: 100%	Yes: 58%	No: 100% Yes: 0%	High: 100% Some: 0% None: 0%	4
Who Is Behind Me?	Yes: 96 %	Yes: 96%	No: 100% Yes: 0%	High: 83% Some: 17% None: 0%	4
Good Evening Moon	Yes: 94%	Yes: 53%	No: 89% Yes: 11%	High: 70% Some: 18% None: 12%	4

23 sentences, and some of those sentences are loosely defined to make up a repetitive pattern throughout the book. For instance, the story opens with the following (Fukuda, 2004, pp. 2–3):

Sentence 1: ぼくの うしろに いるの だあれ [Who is behind me?]
Sentence 2: あっ かめくん [Ah. Turtle.]
Sentence 3: かめくんの うしろに いるの だあれ [Who is behind the turtle?]
Sentence 4: あっ ねこさん [Ah. Cat.]

The story continues with this pattern alternating whether the next animal is behind, in front of, on top of, or below the previous animal.

Emma made four text-initiated switches that showed how she engaged in the reading process when reading the story. These switches were categorized as sequential contrasts, defined as switches that help to organize the conversation for making connections and problem solving around book reading. Three of the four switches were connected to self-corrections related to the graphic information in the text. Reading the first line of the story ぼくの うしろに いるの だあれ [Who is behind me?], Emma inserted the subject marker は (wa) and talked through her understanding of the pronunciation of の (no) in the following manner.

Line 1: Emma read the text, "ぼくの うしろに いる**の は** だあれ" [Who is behind me?].
Line 2: Although Emma pronounced の, she pointed to the form の and said, "I'm thinking what's that letter. の (no)."
Line 3: Emma confirmed her reading of の, reread the text and self-corrected, "ぼくの うしろに いるの だあれ" [Who is behind me?].

While the insertion of は (wa) did not change the meaning of the text in line 1, it resulted in a slight alteration in the nuance of the sentence. Emma most likely predicted that は (wa) would act as a subject marker. At the same time, in her switch in line 2, she pointed to the form の (no) and questioned what the "letter" is. Confirming her reading of の (no), she reread the sentence, and in this process, she also self-corrected the insertion of は (wa) in the sentence to read it as expected.

Emma engaged in another, similar type of switch when reading the last sentence, みんな ちかくに いたんだね [Everyone was there] (Fukuda, 2004, p. 28). The switch played out in the following way, Emma said:

Line 1: Emma read, "みんな **ち** . . ." [Everyone . . .]
Line 2: Emma pointed to ち and said, "Is this chi?"
Line 3: Emma confirmed her predication and read, "みんな ちかくに いたんだ**に . . .**"

Line 4: She stopped reading and said, "No," and self-corrected and read, "ね" (ne).

Here, Emma made two switches, one in line 2 and the other in line 4, to question the graphic information in the text. In the first switch in line 2, she asked, "Is this chi?" to which I did not respond. She confirmed independently and continued reading. For the last switch in line 4, Emma indicated that her prediction of に (ni) for ね (ne) did not make sense and said, "No" to self-correct.

When reading the same book, Emma made one switch that did not result in a self-correction, although she may have intended it to be. In the story, the animals are addressed using a suffix, *kun*, *san*, or *chyan*. These suffixes carry formality and gendered identifications. For instance, *san* or *sama* is the formal way to address an individual when attached to the end of their name or title. The use of *kun* indicates that the person or thing is positioned as a male, used mostly for young children, and *chyan* is used for children and mostly females. For instance, Emma's grandmother called her Emma-chyan. In the story, the turtle is called *kamekun*, which suggests that the turtle is gendered as a young male, and the cat is called *nekosan*, which is a slightly more formal way of calling the cat and not necessarily attached to age. The story uses only *kun* and *san*. Emma, however, substituted all instances of *san* for *chyan*, most likely because it was more in alignment with the use of *kun*.

Emma talked her way through the following sentence, あっ ぞうさん. ぞうさんの まえに いるの だあれ [Ah, elephant. Who is in front of the elephant?] (Fukuda, 2004, p. 8). Emma said,

Line 1: Emma read, "あっ ぞうくん." [Ah . . . elephant-**kun**]
Line 2: Emma stopped reading and said, "Oh! That's not it."
Line 3: Emma unsuccessfully corrected and read, "あっ ぞう**ちゃん**. ぞう**ちゃん**の まえに いるの だあれ." [Ah . . . elephant-**chyan**. Who is in front of elephant-**chyan**?]

In line 1, Emma used *kun* instead of *san* to identify the elephant. However, she disconfirmed her prediction in line 2 and tried to correct it with another graphically similar suffix *chyan* in line 3. Because the use of *chyan* made more sense since it aligned linguistically with the use of *kun* in the story, Emma substituted *chyan* for *kun* throughout the entire story.

Illustrated in the previous examples, Emma's movement out of the written forms of the text served important psycholinguistic functions to confirm or disconfirm her predictions. Her switches, in many ways, acted as a think aloud to problem-solve through the reading process, and the variety of language forms helped organize that dialogue. Through the switches, she questioned not only the Japanese hiragana forms and sounds but also the meaning. As an example, Emma self-corrected に (ni) for ね (ne) because *ne*, while it does not hold a particular semantic meaning, is used at the end of the sentence to provide emphasis. に (ni) serves the grammatical function of a particle, and placing it at the end of the sentence did not make sense.

To provide another example of how code-switching reflected linguistic flexibility in moving between two language forms when reading, Emma code-switched to retell entire stories. Emma read *Kasa* (Matsuno, 1985) with her father. After reading the book, I asked her in English to tell me what the story was about. Because I initiated a participant-related language switch, Emma switched to English in the following dialogue.

> Emma read, "Kasa sashite kaerou." [Lets open the umbrella and go home.]
> "Can you tell me about what you read?" I asked as soon as she finished reading.
> "What about . . . what about . . .," Emma started. "How do you say kasa in English? I know. Umbrella. And everyone has different umbrellas. One is red, one is yellow, one is blue, and one is green and one is white that you can see through and one is blue. One is black and one is rainbow and another red one."

In another example, Emma read *Good Evening Moon* (Hayashi, 1986), which had the lowest miscue statistics, and created one switch. *Good Evening Moon* has 17 sentences and, unlike *Who Is Behind Me?*, lacks a repetitious and predictable pattern. The lack of a pattern appeared to have more impact on her oral reading than her retelling. In a similar way, I asked in English to tell me what the story was about. Emma replied in English and produced a one-word switch: "It was about おつきさま [Mr. Moon] and he got covered by the clouds. The clouds moved so he could see the moon and he was happy again."

Emma's retelling evidenced a one-word switch to Japanese with her use of おつきさま [Mr. Moon]. Unlike her switch when retelling *Kasa* in which she said, "How do you say *kasa* in English?," Emma most likely kept with the language of the text because おつきさま [Mr. Moon] holds a distinctive sociocultural meaning in Japanese, indicated by the use of *sama* at the end of the word *moon*, which is the most formal way to address someone or something. By adding *sama*, the story personifies the moon to a special status that cannot be translated or compared to a singular meaning for the English word *moon*, in the way that *kasa* could be translated to umbrella. As such, Emma prudently kept the language form of the text in her retelling.

While there appears to be a connection between the number of times Emma code-switched during the reading, to work out her ideas and predictions of the text, and her miscue statistics, we cannot generalize that the more bilingual readers switch during reading events, the more effective their reading will be. Book characteristics can impact a beginning reader's oral reading behaviors, such as changes in rhyme and repetition, the level to which the illustrations match the text, and the use of natural rather than controlled language in books. These characteristics likely played a role in Emma's abilities to predict and confirm texts. Her bilingual language behaviors, however, were important indicators of the complexity to which novice bilingual readers approach reading as a process of inquiry and problem solving.

Code-switching can be viewed as a verbal tool that allowed Emma to not only accomplish an immediate, situated activity by finding a solution to a problem that she encountered. Emma was also able to code-switch for tactical conversational moves, such as changing the topic, addressing the language of other participants, and emphasizing points that she wanted to make as she engaged in the reading process (Kabuto, 2010). These short-term goals developed Emma's linguistic repertoire as well as developed her reading ability. While this may be the case, long-term social consequences evolved out of these daily interactions with language, texts, and individuals in her environment that constructed her identity as a bilingual reader.

Jenny: A Profile of Code-Switching Over Time

Jenny's Profile reflects two points in time to document the changes in her bilingual reading behaviors. I first met Jenny when I worked with her older brother Thomas, whom readers met in Chapter 2. At that time, Jenny was 5 years old, and Thomas was 12 and in the sixth grade. Maria and Thomas enjoyed reading to Jenny, and she thoroughly loved listening to stories. She would carry a small backpack around with paper, pencils, crayons, and books, and when she brought a book to her mom, Maria would open the book to begin reading. At one point, when Maria explained that Jenny often asked Thomas to read to her, Jenny immediately responded, "No sé cómo leer los cuentos" [I don't know how to read stories.] Maria, in an encouraging way, responded to Jenny that she would learn to read and mentioned one of her favorite books about puppies.

As Thomas described for his Profile, acquiring books written in Spanish was a challenge. Thomas, as a result, read books to Jenny in either language even if the book was written in English. Jenny was aware of this flexible use of language, and Thomas described how Jenny read books "using the pictures to tell the story." Like other 5-year-olds, Jenny liked having the same book read to her each night before bed, and Thomas noted that one of the stories she read using the pictures was *Peanut Butter Rhino* (Andriani, 1994). When I asked Jenny to share and read the book to me, she exhibited effective beginning reading behaviors characteristic of novice bilingual readers (Goodman et al., 2007). Table 4.2 outlines and compares Jenny's reading of *Peanut Butter Rhino* with the written text.

Jenny began the story with a clearly defined story structure using story language, "Hoy es el día que yo voy a visitar a mi amigo elefante" [Today is the day that I am going to visit my elephant friend] and continued to bring story elements into her reading of the story. For instance, using the pictures, she provided the names of the items in the lunch box: *mantequilla de maní y mermelada* [peanut butter and jelly], *una banana* [banana], and *una manzana*

Table 4.2 Jenny's Reading of Peanut Butter Rhino at 5 Years

Page Numbers	*Story Text*	*Jenny's Reading*	*English Translation*
3	Today is the day that I have lunch with my good friend Elephant.	Hoy es el dia que yo voy a visitar a mi amigo elefante.	Today is the day that I am going to visit my elephant friend.
4–5	I'll just check my lunchbox to make sure I didn't forget anything. Let me see . . . a delicious peanut butter sandwich, and apple, some carrots, and a banana. Okay. Everything's here.	Voy a revisar a ver si tengo todo. Ok. Un sandwich de mantiquilla de mani marmelada. Una zanahoria, una banana, una manzana. Ok. Esta todo.	I'm going to check to make sure I have everything. Okay. One peanut butter jelly sandwich. One carrot. One carrot. One banana. One apple. Okay. Everything is here.
6–7	Hey, where's my peanut butter sandwich? My sandwich has got to be around here somewhere. Maybe it's under this rock.	¿Donde esta mi sandwich de mantiquilla de mani marmelada? Tal vez esta abajo de esta roca? No.	Where is my peanut butter jelly sandwich? Maybe it is under this rock. No.
8–9	Monkey, have you seen my peanut butter sandwich? No, I haven't, Rhino. It's not up in this tree.	Han visto mi sandwich de mantiquilla de mani marmelada? No, no lo visto. Pero yo te voy a ayudar encontrarla.	Have you seen my peanut butter jelly sandwich? No. I haven't but I will help you find it.
10–11	Lion, have you seen my peanut butter sandwich? No, I haven't Rhino. But I will help you look for it. It's not in this cave. No sandwich in this tree either.	Han visto un sandwich de mantequilla de mani marmelada? No, no lo visto. Pero yo te voy a ayudar encontrarla.	Have you seen a peanut butter jelly sandwich? No, I haven't seen it, but I will help you find it.
12–13	Sorry Rhino, there's no peanut butter sandwich here. Just some old cheese. It's no use. I've lost it. I'll just have to go see elephant without my most wonderful peanut butter sandwich.	Si yo no tengo un sandwich de mantequilla de mani marmelada, como voy a llevar a adonde mi amigo no canta?	If I don't have a peanut butter jelly sandwich then how will be able to go . . . my friend does not sing.
14–15	Excuse me, Rhino. Why is there a squished peanut butter sandwich on your bottom? Squished?	Dice: Porque tienes un sandwich aplastada a su trasero? Porque tienes un sandwich aplastado.	Why is there a squished sandwich on your behind? Why do you have a squished . . . squished sandwich?
16	Good thing I brought two peanut butter sandwiches. One for me and one for you! Hooray!	Que bueno que traiste dos. Uno para mi y otro para ti.	How great that you brought two. One for me and one for you.

[apple], and the problem in the story, which was that Rhino could not find his peanut butter sandwich and had to ask the other animals if they knew the location of the sandwich.

After reading the book, Jenny and I engaged in the following dialogue:

Line 1: Jenny read, "Qué bueno que trajiste dos. Uno para mí y otro para ti." [How nice that you brought two. One for me and one for you.]
Line 2: "Jenny, where was that peanut butter sandwich?," I asked.
Line 3: "Trasero!" [Rearend!]
Line 4: "Thank you for sharing the book, Jenny," I said.
Line 5: "You're welcome," Jenny said.

Our conversation presents an additional type of code-switch: a change in the mode of interaction. I made the first switch in line 2, when I tried to change the mode of interaction by asking Jenny where Rhino found the peanut butter sandwich in English, my preferred language of communication. Jenny initiated the second switch in line 3 for similar reasons when she said, "Trasero!"

As a participant in the reading event, I recognized Jenny's constructed text. So, her use of the word *tresero* was a natural response to my question. After her response, I made another switch in line 4 to English thanking her for reading the book, to which Jenny responded, "You're welcome." My switch was successful in changing the mode of the interaction and prompted Jenny to make a switch in her response.

As this reading event illustrates, Jenny's language preference leaned toward Spanish; she was undoubtedly more comfortable using Spanish to speak and read. Although Jenny stated early on that she did not know how to read, she demonstrated effective novice bilingual reading behaviors and a certain linguistic flexibility as she drew from picture cues in the book to create a discourse rich with story language and details. Her reading included the characters, setting, story events, problem, and resolution. Furthermore, by employing embodied reading behaviors, she physically acted and sounded like a reader, leading individuals listening to the story without previewing the book to believe that the book was possibly written in Spanish.

Two and a half years later, Jenny was 8 years old and in the second grade in a dual-language school. She was more bilingually conversant and had transitioned from being a novice reader to an independent bilingual reader. She expressed that she liked to read across linguistically diverse texts and felt herself a good reader whether in English or Spanish. When asked if there were an area where she would like to improve as a reader, Jenny said that she would like to improve in reading English texts because she had difficulty with some words, which she associated with being better prepared to do well on the New York State testing in English Language Arts. Jenny said, "When I take a test in English, there are some words that I can't understand." She followed up by saying, "In Spanish, I know all the words." The connection between knowing the words and being a good reader was an area of reading Jenny referenced when talking about effective reading. When asked who was a good reader that she knew, for instance, Jenny said that her class friend was a good reader because "she knows all the words in English and Spanish."

Jenny read three books as part of the second-grade portion of her Profile. Table 4.3 outlines the miscue statistics and retelling scores for the three books. In addition to reading *Alexander and the Wind-Up Mouse* (Lionni, 1969), Jenny revisited the book *Peanut Butter Rhino*. She was excited to see the book and did not remember reading it to me or having the book read to her at home. Jenny explained,

> Because when I didn't see you, I was practicing to read. When I was in first grade, I had a test to read. I had to read in front of a lot of people, and I needed to read, so I practiced this book [*Peanut Butter Rhino*] at home. I brought this to school and read it.

Jenny, however, made the following comment before reading the book: "And the elephant's gonna see that it's on her butt," suggesting her familiarity with the book. Jenny read one Spanish text, *Jack y los frijoles mágicos* [*Jack and the Beanstalk*].

Across the three books, Jenny worked at reading *Alexander and the Wind-Up Mouse* as demonstrated by the number of nonwords resulting in sentences with meaning loss. For instance, she read *squeak* as /squeetch/ and *rustled* as /rushled/. The lower percentage of sentences that made sense, however, did not impact her ability to retell the story. When asked to retell the story, Jenny said,

Table 4.3 Miscue Analysis Data for Jenny at 7 Years (Second Grade)

Books	*Syntactic Acceptability*	*Semantic Acceptability*	*Meaning Change*	*Graphic Similarity*	*Retelling Score*
English Books					
Peanut Butter Rhino	Yes: 96%	Yes: 93%	No: 100% Yes: 0%	High: 100% Some: 0% None: 0%	4.0
Alexander and the Wind-Up Mouse	Yes: 94 %	Yes: 79%	No: 98% Yes: 0%	High: 81% Some: 15% None: 4%	4.0
Spanish Books					
Jack and the Beanstalk	Yes: 98%	Yes: 98%	No: 98% Yes: 0%	High: 67% Some: 33% None: 0%	4.0

> Alexander a normal mouse and then he met a new friend, but he wasn't normal. He had a key and wheel. But Alexander had feet so Alexander . . . there was a lizard. So the lizard said to Alexander to bring him a purple pebble. So Alexander did it, but when the magic did it . . . when Alexander went to the box, it was empty. He thought that the magic didn't work. He went to his hole and he find Willy. That's how the story ends.

She received an overall retelling score of 4, suggesting that she understood the range of elements in the story structure.

Conversely, Jenny read *Jack and the Beanstalk* with a high percentage of grammatically and semantically acceptable sentences. She also received a high retelling score. Unlike in her retelling of *Alexander and the Wind-Up Mouse* and *Peanut Butter Rhino*, Jenny engaged in code-switching behaviors when retelling *Jack and the Beanstalk*. After reading the story, the retelling unfolded in the following way:

Line 1: Livia asked, "What was the story about, Jenny?"

Line 2: Jenny replied, "The story was about a boy named Jack and his mother were poor and her mother sent him to get some money because she wanted to sell the cow so then when Jack went to sell the cow there was a little man so the man said that he would buy the cow. The man said how are you going to pay and Jack said that he will pay with some magic beans. Jack gave the man the magic beans and took the cow home. Jack gave the beans to her mom but her mom didn't want the beans, her mom wanted money so the mom threw the beans out of the house and then the other morning when Jack woke up, his room was so dark that Jack opened the window and saw a big . . . a big . . ."

Line 3: "Tell me in Spanish," Livia said.

Line 4: Jenny replied, "Un tallo gigante." [a giant stem].

Line 5: Jenny continued the retelling, "And then Jack climbed and climbed until he got to the castle. So then he touched the door and there was a woman that opened him the door and the woman told him that there was a big giant that ate kids so then Jack said that he only wanted to get money so then the woman let him in and the giant came and the woman hid Jack and the giant smelled the kid and Jack was so scared so when the giant go to sleep, he got out and he walked and then . . . and then . . ."

Line 6: Maria responded, "Si no puedes decirlo en español." [If you can't say it in Spanish.]

Line 7: Livia confirmed, "Yeah, si no puedes decirlo en español." [If you can't say it in Spanish.]

Line 8: Jenny continued in Spanish, "Caminó de puntitas. El gigante se despertó y Jack corrió e dijo a la mamá que pase el hacha para cortar el tallo y el gigante murió cuando se cayó y Jack y su mamá fueron ricos para siempre." [He walked on his tippy toes. The giant awoke and Jack ran and told his mom to pass the ax to cut the stem and the giant died when he fell and Jack and his mom were rich forever.]

Jenny switched three times in the retelling, in lines 4, 5, and 8. The first switch, occurring in line 4 and initiated by Livia, was a switch that changed the mode of interaction as Livia engaged in a process of in-the-moment assessment. Rather than provide Jenny the word or prompt her with questions, Livia determined that Jenny was having a difficult time explaining the story in English and encouraged her to use Spanish. Jenny switched to *un tallo gigante* [a giant stem] and initiated a switch back to English in Line 5. Maria switched in line 6 following Livia's lead, which was taken up by both Livia and Jenny in line 7, and Jenny seamlessly continued her telling in Spanish.

These switches were critical for Jenny to communicate her understanding of the text. Livia and Maria felt that Jenny knew the information and needed to draw on her bilingualism to retell the story. As they evaluated and observed Jenny, they acknowledged that Jenny needed to draw from all the resources available to her when retelling the story, particularly a story written in Spanish. Terms that Jenny used, like *un tallo gigante* [a giant stem] and *caminó de puntitas* [walked on tippy toes], were not directly in the story. Jenny's understanding of the story was deeper than the written text and required that she draw on Spanish forms to express the deep meaning that she constructed when reading.

Jenny's switches were constructed in natural changes in the mode of the linguistic interactions and had evolved over time between 5 and 8 years old. In both points in time, Jenny demonstrated flexible use of language, and this flexibility allowed her to move between the written language of text and her language preference. At 5 years, she read in Spanish the story written in English, and even when I asked her in English about the story, she stayed with Spanish. As Jenny became an independent reader, she aligned her oral reading with the written text and drew from her language flexibility when retelling the story.

Lesson Learned From the Profiles

The two Profiles illustrate the synergy that existed among the translanguaging context, reading events, and linguistic interactions giving a socially constructed nature to Emma's and Jenny's reading performances. The conversational moves added another layer to the miscue statistics to illustrate the strategic manner in which the readers engaged in reading as a meaning-making process. The miscue statistics, in the end and notwithstanding their contribution to understanding reading as a transactive process, are quantitative measures of reading performances that did little to document the accompanying dialogue and shifts that acted as additional windows into the reading process. Minimizing the intentional ways that bilingual readers navigate and tactically use language as a verbal tool to seamlessly draw from a gamut of linguistic forms to problem-solve with text is determinantal for novice bilingual readers and promotes a deficit view of how linguistically diverse novice readers approach reading.

Emma's Profile, for instance, elucidates how her use of linguistic forms was connected to how she engaged in the reading process. The switching between English and Japanese forms helped Emma organize the reading event to reflect an inquiry-based approach to transacting with texts. She read the text in Japanese, the expected form, and then switched to English when she needed to confirm or disconfirm her predictions. Emma's behavior contributes to the many documented code-switching purposes in educational contexts that view code-switching as a problem-solving technique for young bilingual speakers as they try to comprehend academic content and discourses (Cahyani et al., 2018; Karlsson, 2016). Emma's switching in language forms suggests that it can be a vital linguistic interaction permitting readers to solve problems with texts.

Conversely, Jenny tried to fashion distinct boundaries as reflected in her initial retelling in English of *Jack and the Beanstalk*. Because she began her retelling in English, she most likely wanted to stay in that mode, as indicated by her switch back to English after saying *un tallo gigante* [a giant stem]. Jenny's use of *un tallo gigante*, like Emma's use of Japanese words from the text, was not about a lack of English vocabulary. Rather, selecting which mode to use was demonstrative of how certain meanings were not translatable and held very specific sociocultural meanings that could only be represented in the language form readers deemed more appropriate. Not drawing from all their linguistic resources would have limited their ability to retell the story.

In Jenny's case, however, Maria and Livia viewed her as a knowledgeable independent reader, and the more they viewed her as such, the more they encouraged her to switch to communicate her understanding. The type of feedback that Maria and Livia provided was the direct result of having watched, observed, and assessed, moment to moment, not only Jenny's reading progress and language competence but also her evolving identity. As other studies have shown, with children as young as 2 years old, family members and teachers will adjust their language based on the language preference of the interlocutor (Comeau et al., 2003; Flores-Ferrán & Suh, 2015). This adjustment changes over time based on the purpose of the dialogue and the developing language proficiency of the child. With a 5-year-old who was exhibiting a preference to speak Spanish, Livia, Maria, Thomas, and I acknowledged this and did not urge switches. When Jenny was 8 years old, however, the participants became strategic partners that aided not only the construction of the translanguaging space but also the actualizing of Jenny's identity as an independent bilingual reader.

While both Jenny and Emma were considered novice bilingual readers, they did not use language forms in the same way or for the same purpose at any moment or over time. This created a situation in which the translanguaging space was not stable or consistent as the reading events were developed through language. The negotiation of linguistic forms provided a map to examine how the context evolved from event to event and at two different points in time. The end goal was that novice bilingual readers were supported as they demonstrated their reading abilities and identities.

References

Andriani, V. (1994). *Peanut butter rhino*. Scholastic.

Cahyani, H., de Courcy, M., & Barnett, J. (2018). Teachers' code-switching in bilingual classrooms: Exploring pedagogical and sociocultural functions. *International Journal of Bilingual Education and Bilingualism*, *21*(4), 465–479.

Comeau, L., Genesee, F., & Lapaquette, L. (2003). The modeling hypothesis and child bilingual codemixing. *International Journal of Bilingualism*, 7(2), 113–126.

Cummins, J. (2017). Teaching minoritized students: Are additive approaches legitimate? *Harvard Educational Review*, *87*(3), 404–425.

Flores-Ferrán, N., & Suh, S. (2015). A case study of a Korean-American family's code switching during conflict-related interaction. *Journal of Language Aggression and Conflict*, *3*(2), 289–316.

Fukuda, T. (2004). *Ushiro ni iru no dare*. Shinpusha.

Goodman, D., Flurkey, A., & Goodman, Y. (2007). Effective young beginning readers. In Y. Goodman & P. Martens (Eds.), *Critical issues in early literacy*. Lawrence Erlbaum.

Gumperz, J. (1982). *Discourse strategies*. Cambridge University Press.

Hayashi, A. (1986). *Otsukisama konbawa*. Fukuinkan Shoten.

Heller, M. (1988). Strategic ambiguity: Codeswitching in the management of conflict. In M. Heller (Ed.), *Codeswitching: Anthropological and sociolinguistic perspectives* (pp. 77–96). Mouton de Gruyter.

Kabuto, B. (2010). Code-switching during parent-child reading interactions: Taking multiple theoretical perspectives. *Journal of Early Childhood Literacy*, *10*(2), 131–157.

Karlsson, A. (2016). Code-switching as a linguistic resource in the multilingual science classroom. In *11th Conference of the European Science Education Research Association (ESERA), Helsinki, Finland* (pp. 1820–1831). University of Helsinki.

Lemke, J. (2000). Across the scales of time: Artifacts, activities, and meanings in ecosocial systems. *Mind, Culture, and Activity*, 7(4), 273–290.

Lionni, L. (1969). *Alexander and the wind-up mouse*. Dragonfly Books.

MacSwan, J. (2017). A multilingual perspective on translanguaging. *American Educational Research Journal*, *54*(1), 167–201.

Matsuno, M. (1985). *Kasa*. Fukuinkan Shoten.

Otheguy, R., García, O., & Reid, W. (2019). A translanguaging view of the linguistic system of bilinguals. *Applied Linguistics Review*, *10*(4), 625–651.

Poza, L. (2017). Translanguaging: Definitions, implications, and further needs in burgeoning inquiry. *Berkeley Review of Education*, *6*(2), 101–128.

Rogers, H. (2005). *Writing systems: A linguistic approach*. Blackwell Publishing.

Ryan, P. M. (2005). *Yo, Naomi Leon* (N. Molinero, Trans.). Scholastic en Espanol.

Verhoeven, L. T. W., & Perfetti, C. A. (2017). Introduction: Operating principles in learning to read. In L. Verhoeven & C. Perfetti (Eds.), *Learning to read across languages and writing systems* (pp. 1–30). Cambridge University Press.

Wei, L. (2011). Moment analysis and translanguaging space: Discursive construction of identities by multilingual Chinese youth in Britain. *Journal of Pragmatics*, *43*(5), 1222–1235.

Wei, L., & Lin, A. M. (2019). Translanguaging classroom discourse: Pushing limits, breaking boundaries. *Classroom Discourse*, *10*(3–4), 209–215.

Yow, W. Q., Tan, J. S., & Flynn, S. (2018). Code-switching as a marker of linguistic competence in bilingual children. *Bilingualism: Language and Cognition*, *21*(5), 1075–1090.

5 Profiles of Bilingual Reading Identities and Abilities

Returning to Sophie's and Jenny's Profiles, this chapter will further explore the social origins of bilingual reading abilities and how they connect to identity in the third section of the Profiles: Biliteracy Manifestations. Drawing from the work of Whitmore and Meyer (2020), the term *biliterate manifestations* refers to the "stuff," ranging from reading, storying, drawing, writing, and reflecting, that bilingual readers produce as they engage in bilingual reading events and practices. Manifestations are the artifacts that result from doing and, as such, embody complex notions of ability and are windows into identity. This idea is supported by other conceptualizations of identity. The work of Rowsell and Pahl (2007), for instance, described identity as sedimented, meaning identities can be evidenced in texts, and by studying the texts, we can a get glimpse of the multiple, discursive selves that emerge from practice.

Biliteracy manifestations bring the data together to create the narrative of how becoming bilingual and biliterate is consequential to one's participation in the local – bilingual reading events, family practices, and educational structures – as the local interacts with more global and invisible social and ideological processes of power and domination. The ways in which bilingual reading identities transverse local and global processes reveal that becoming biliterate is not unidimensional. Linguistically diverse individuals can develop intricate aspects of their identities that can conflict and support each other when situated in different contexts.

Socially Constructed Identities and Abilities Within a Translanguaging Context

Language, learning, and identity are intricately entangled concepts, complex and layered, that are inseparable from who we are and who we want to become as human beings (Packer & Goicoechea, 2000; Whitmore & Meyer, 2020). Gee (2004) described identity as a kit of "ways of being in the world" and how we learn to be different types of "culturally-specific" people through a broad range of tools (such as language, books, and writing materials), while performing different types of behaviors (acting, dressing,

DOI: 10.4324/9781003045984-6

and talking) and expressing feelings and values (frustration, embarrassment, and pride). "Being in the world," however, is not the same as "becoming in the world." The process of becoming a bilingual reader, therefore, involves the doing (reading, reflecting, and discussing) of literacy practices, and, as readers interact with others, they learn what it means to be not just a bilingual reader but also biliterate.

To define and conceptualize identity, I will draw from Holland et al. (1998) to discuss identity as the collective aspects of personal and social selves that are "lived in and through activity and so must be conceptualized as they develop in social practice" (p. 5). In order to locate identities within social practice, Holland et al. (1998) provide two interconnected concepts – self-in-action (the doing) and sense-of-self (the telling or storying) – that help conceptualize the personal and social aspects of identity construction.

Self-in-action is how readers actualize themselves through their literacy practices and can be observed and documented in literacy events. The Profiles of Sophie, Jenny, Emma, and Mai in Chapters 3 and 4 are examples of how these bilingual readers engaged in the reading process and reflected on their reading performances. Chapter 3 focused on Sophie's and Mai's bilingual reading enactments by documenting and analyzing their miscues and retellings. Chapter 4 added another dimension to understanding self-in-action through code-switching and language behaviors as co-constructed by others who participated in the events to support story comprehension.

In Chapter 4, Emma's negotiation and fluid movement among linguistic forms illustrated how she actively engaged in bilingual reading events. Through her participation, Emma enacted her identity through language as constitutive of the translanguaging context. The addition of a code-switching lens reinforced the argument that the movement among linguistic forms was the result of language competence to problem-solve difficult areas. More importantly, these localized self-in-action enactments negotiated Emma's bilingual reading identities.

While each reader in this book may or may not have been cognizant of the linguistic choices they made, they nonetheless used various linguistic tools and discursive practices to make decisions on the affordances and limitations of their choices in accomplishing the task at hand. Each choice that the readers made, like Jenny's decision to retell *Jack and the Beanstalk* in English, was mediated by the people and the materials, like books, present in the context. No decision or display of bilingual reading behaviors was neutral – each one communicated the kind of person the reader wanted or intended to be. These behaviors were further contextualized through the ways that the readers storied their everyday, biliterate lives, resulting in the documentation of behaviors and artifacts (miscues, retellings, reflections, and interviews) that were manifestations of a translanguaging context.

Assessments, like high-stakes testing and some common classroom-based evaluations of reading related to leveling, give the false impression that there is a single ability seen through the lens of a White, monolingual norm (Willis, 2019). While many teachers and parents may agree that such assessments cannot capture the range of reading behaviors – particularly for linguistically diverse students – teachers, administrators, and parents alike still privilege and default to the information they provide to measure students' reading performance. These types of assessments may result in inaccurate and toxic outcomes and literacies (Ellis & Smith, 2017; Taylor, 1996).

From this perspective, bilingual reading identities and abilities are circuitously connected, as they are mediated by people – teachers or parents – and tools in the environment – books and tests. As bilingual readers read, their reading performances are observed and judged by educators and parents who place value and privilege on certain types of behaviors – a common theme that I have tried to emphasize throughout this book. Bilingual reading abilities are thus not a predefined standard notion but rather are defined and constructed as readers engage in the act of reading, as they themselves, as well as others, interpret what it means to be a bilingual reader.

As an example, the negotiation, refinement, and acceptance of Emma's language behaviors over time supported her identity in her early biliteracy. Reading within a translanguaging context provided Emma with the linguistic tools that she needed to participate in reading events with Japanese texts. At the same time, the ways that Emma employed language and how that employment was accepted or rejected at home linked up to larger possibilities for Emma to take on multiple roles and develop relationships with others through the use of language. While Emma's language choices were verbal acts, they were also social actions and reactions to other people around her. This point is illustrated through the ways in which code-switching evolved and changed over time.

As Emma was in the process of becoming an independent bilingual reader, her language behaviors demonstrated more linguistic fluidity. At this young age, Emma was still an early beginning reader and naturally trying to make sense of linguistically diverse texts through the integration of semantic, syntactic, and graphophonic information as illustrated in Chapter 4. Many of Emma's switches reflected this behavior. As I presented earlier, Emma switched from the language of the text, Japanese, to say things like "I don't need that" when something did not make sense or self-monitored her reading by saying, "No" or "I don't know."

Over time, however, as bilingual readers develop more effective and independent ways to engage in the reading process, the dynamic relationships that they have with other reading participants, particularly parents, begin to shift. Instead of Emma's dad reading to Emma, he started to encourage her to read, which gave Emma more freedom and control in the conversation. Maria, similarly, shifted her language interactions and expectations with Jenny over time as Maria observed and supported Jenny as a reader and engaged with Jenny in strategic ways as Maria assessed Jenny from moment to moment.

Parents, therefore, pass over more reading responsibility to their children, which provides them with a space to take more control and negotiate the translanguaging context. The shifting roles in social relationships result in ambiguity, which requires parents to reinterpret and react to new situations (Heller, 1988). Both parents and their children perceive events, relate them to what they already know, and act in ways that access them power and acceptance into relationships with other people. As parents modify their roles, they co-construct their children's identities as bilingual readers and these modifications of roles become reflected in the evolving nature of the translanguaging context.

The self-in-action acts in tandem with one's sense-of-self. Sense-of-self refers to how individuals personally position themselves within social contexts and with other people. Bilingual readers like those in this book do not operate in isolation from the social context. The sense-of-self is influenced by how others orient themselves to other individuals or how tools are used to mediate the meaning-making processes. Jenny, for instance, read *Peanut Butter Rhino* in Spanish when she was 5 years old and presented herself as a novice Spanish reader. She also began developing a sense of herself as a bilingual reader, as Livia, Maria, and I responded to her reading behaviors. In second grade, Jenny told a different story of her experiences of reading *Peanut Butter Rhino* relating that she needed to read the book in English in first grade and practiced the book at home in order to read it at school. At two different points in time, the same book brought out two different reading actions that resulted in Jenny shifting from a novice bilingual reader to an independent reader who began associating reading in English with formal reading and language instruction.

For Emma, while her reader identity was constructed through transacting with Japanese and English texts, she also needed to redefine and articulate her social and language identities. If Emma did not see herself as a speaker of Japanese, she would not have seen herself as a competent and capable bilingual reader. The translanguaging context was a way for Emma to work across language boundaries to develop not only those competencies, but also to see herself in the roles of reader and language user. In this sense, Emma's and Jenny's local uses, acceptances, or rejections of language forms have long-term consequences in how they perceive their participation and ability as readers.

Jenny's and Emma's language choices involved "recognition work" (Gee, 1996) that is required in the process of becoming biliterate. This type of work encapsulates developing relationships with others, such as their teachers, classmates, or parents, who interpret their actions and respond to them in ways that recognize them as bilingual readers or not. There are times when bilingual readers try to align with the language behaviors of the people and context, there are times when they do not, and there are times when they may do a little of both. Again, this type of recognition work evolves from moment-to-moment over shorter or longer timescales as bilingual readers talk about reading and talk about themselves as bilingual readers. During these acts, tensions, inconsistencies, and continuities between the "telling" and "doing" can be sites of identity contestations that result in subtle to overt acceptance or rejection of linguistic forms that make up the artifactual stuff that represents meaning.

The Profiles given in the following will explore further the relationships between reading abilities and identities, as well as how they were socially constructed over time within the family. The goal is to envision how becoming a bilingual reader was part of a larger process of becoming biliterate, which was a process of struggle and contestation over time and across home and school contexts. As the tools and contexts evolved, so did the process of becoming biliterate. The tools and context were constitutive of one another and unique to each reader and family as they constructed their own understanding of what it means to be biliterate through the ongoing and never-ending process of becoming biliterate through the doing and telling.

Sophie: Biliterate Manifestations of Contestation

Chapter 3 focused on the observations of Sophie's bilingual reading behaviors and documented the reflective and collaborative conversations about her miscues to illustrate her cognizance of the diverse ways she approached reading in Greek and English. Within a socially and linguistically constructed translanguaging context, meaning was the driving force behind her high-quality miscues and self-corrections. At various instances, she balanced meaning with her language experiences, grammar, and graphic information. Regardless of the text level of the books she read, Sophie exhibited a self-awareness of her reading behaviors and developed discourses to talk about why she made miscues that did not necessarily isolate such reading behaviors as sounding out words, reading too fast, or asking for assistance. Sophie's observations in this regard, however, did not always coincide with how she talked about herself as a bilingual reader. The narrative that Sophie created was one in which there were separate reading abilities, one for English and one for Greek, and they competed and were measured against each other by her mother Frances.

Sophie felt that she was a "good reader" and clearly articulated her preference for reading in English. She explained during the initial interview, "I know how to read Greek, but I don't want to read Greek books." Sophie's mother Frances supported Sophie's preference for reading in English and explained that she read English books to Sophie when she was younger. Frances was not concerned that Sophie had little interest in reading in Greek because she could speak Greek, and she said that "bilingualism is an asset." Nevertheless, her actions and reflective discussions implied an opinion of English as the more valuable asset holding a privileged position among languages.

Explaining how she had learned to read in English, Sophie said, "I think that I would hear my mom read and I would try to read easy books and then I would go more advanced." She discussed a different method for learning to read in Greek:

> I have these Greek books and since I do Greek, I know how to speak Greek. And since I have a few Greek books and I might just look at them and stories that I like I would read them.

Through her discussion, Sophie connected the ability to read in English as part of a family practice. While still connected to the home, learning to read in Greek, however, was described as a more independent, exploratory practice for Sophie.

Speaking in Greek held more importance for both Sophie and Frances because of its connections to family, particularly Sophie's grandmother, and community. Sophie said, "I live in [city name] somewhere around here. I know how to speak Greek because my mom is born from Greece and she taught me how to speak." Sophie's knowledge of Greek, in fact, was an important self-monitoring tool when she read in Greek and would describe her miscues in Greek as "sounding better" or being more "comfortable" with certain ways of reading the text. For instance, Sophie substituted the nonword **πολάμβαναν** for **απολάμβαναν (enjoyed)** and self-corrected the miscue in the sentence, "Ενώ **απολάμβαναν** ένα απλό αλλά πολύ νόστιμο σπιτικό φαγητό ο ποντικός της πόλης μιλούσε για τη γεμάτη πολυτέλεια ζωή του" ["But they enjoyed a simple yet delicious home cooked meal, the city mouse spoke about his full luxurious life."] When asked why she self-corrected, Sophie responded, "Somehow it (her first response) did not sound right."

Her knowledge of Greek was also evidenced by her miscues when reading the English book *The Garden of Abdul Gasazi*. Sophie read the sentence, "Lights were on and he knew that she must be home" as "Lights were open . . ." and then self-corrected to the expected sentence. She explained her miscue as, "That is how you say it in Greek." Frances, however, criticized the dynamic way that Sophie drew from language resources when she listened to and reflected on Sophie's miscue. Frances confirmed that she used the term "open the lights" with Sophie when they were home and blamed herself for Sophie's miscues, explaining, "It could be my mistake. I know it's not the right way a lot of times, and she will ask me, 'Mom, can you close the lights' when she goes to bed instead of 'turn off the lights.'"

Frances also supported Sophie's position and perception of herself as a reader in Greek. Frances reflected on Sophie's reading of *The Mouse of the Countryside and the City Mouse*.

> It was great, you know, but Greek books are not her thing. We don't read as many Greek books as we do English books. Her reading in Greek is not, I mean, whatever her level in English reading, it's not the same. For me, it makes sense. Even though we have a lot of Greek books at home, she always prefers English, and she wanted me to read to her in English.

Frances was particularly interested in how reading fell into levels, and she used levels to benchmark reading abilities. After reading *The Hare and His Friends*, Frances said, "Overall, it's (her Greek reading) is not at whatever her English reading level is. It's definitely below that. I mean her flow when she speaks is fine. You know. But the reading is not, you know . . ." Frances, at the same time, questioned Sophie's reading level in English. She commented on the overall reading performance of *The Garden of Abdul Gasazi*, "I don't have a comparison of other kids her age so I don't know what level she is, but I think she's okay, I think." While Sophie's Profile illustrates that the translanguaging context reflected a range of bilingual reading behaviors, as described in Chapter 3, Frances compared Sophie's reading ability in one language to the other, creating an adverse situation in which reading across languages was seen as competitive.

At the end of our sessions, Sophie and I revisited conversations about herself as a reader. She explained that she did not feel that she was a good reader in Greek, as she did when reading English. She elaborated on her response by stating:

> I'm not too good (at reading in Greek) because I have some Greek books at home, but I sometimes I might just look at them . . . look through the pages. The books in school are a bit hard with the words. They might be a bit confusing. I have trouble pronouncing the words.

Sophie explained that she understood English better and had less difficulty with the words. More striking was Sophie's response when I asked what she learned about herself as a reader through our sessions together: "I kind of sometimes slow down if I'm reading too fast because sometimes when I read with my mom too fast she tells me to slow down or I go back and read the word correctly."

The final interview with Sophie captured how she identified her sense of being a good reader as being aligned with school-based notions of reading ability. Her perception of being a good reader meant knowing and pronouncing the words and reading accurately. Being a Greek reader was not about reading the books at home but rather reading in Greek in school. For Sophie, the books that she read in English and Greek did not match each other in levels, and she felt that she was only a good reader when she read higher level books.

Although the reading events that were part of her Profile were situated in a translanguaging context, Sophie and Frances did not view the diverse linguistic actions within the translanguaging context as a resource or a demonstrated strength. Rather, they divided language into comparable units to define bilingual reading abilities as contestable. Through this process, both mother and daughter rejected the potential that Sophie showed as a bilingual reader.

Jenny: Biliterate Manifestations of Coherence

Jenny's evolving bilingual reading behaviors as she shifted from being a novice to an independent bilingual reader were highlighted in Chapter 4. At 5 years old, Jenny's language behaviors demonstrated many valued early reading behaviors. As time went on, by the time she was 8 years old, her language behaviors shifted to support her transition to an independent reader. The fluid and dynamic ways she engaged in language from moment to moment supported and was supported by her feelings of herself as a bilingual reader to create coherence between her actions and her sense of herself as a bilingual reader.

At 8 years old, Jenny considered herself a good reader and defined that as someone who "likes to make stories." She did not differentiate her abilities as a Spanish or an English reader and thought she was effective regardless of the language. When asked if she would like to be a better reader in Spanish or English, however, Jenny responded, "I think in English because I take a test in English, there are some words that I can't understand. In Spanish, I know all the words." This interpretation of herself was actualized when reading *Jack and the Beanstalk*. When retelling the story, Jenny switched to Spanish to describe how Jack climbed up a giant stem [un tallo gigante] and walked on his tippy toes [caminó de puntitas]. Linking Jenny's comments with her language behaviors supports the view that assessments that limit the language resources not only limit the knowledge that readers can communicate but also how bilingual readers view themselves as readers in relation to assessment practices.

The link between being a good reader and knowing the words was a theme throughout Jenny's reflections. She noted that a classmate was a good reader because she "knows all the words in English and Spanish" and "she never has trouble." When I asked her to elaborate, she criticized her classmate, saying,

> She speaks so low no one can hear her. Today, our teacher said to present something about a boy (in a story) and his actions and words and how he's jealous. We didn't hear her and I just hear her talking a little.

Jenny's perceptions of this particular student may have less to do with knowing all the words – she pointed out that it was difficult to hear the student talk – and more to do with what Jenny *thinks* good readers should have or know.

During our reflective discussions, Jenny and I discussed her high-quality miscues in which she omitted the word *happy* in the sentence, "The two friends spent many ***happy*** hours together." Jenny said that the omission "doesn't matter because if you take out the word *happy* it (the sentence) still makes sense." Yet, she said that she should have self-corrected the sentence by describing, "If I was reading with another teacher, I think that should read all the words. Because if I didn't read, I wouldn't be a better reader." Finding this comment compelling, I asked Jenny why reading with me was different, to which she responded, "Because when I skip some words reading with you, I feel okay because no one says anything to me."

Jenny's comments illustrate that being a reader depends on the context. Although she attended a dual-language school, translanguaging was not a practice in the school. Instead, languages were artificially separated by days so that English and Spanish instructions alternated every other day. This structure was organized by the type of teacher (e.g., English teacher or Spanish teacher) and curriculum (e.g., English books and homework or Spanish books and homework) and followed a language separation and alternative language approach. The dual-language context, in other words, perpetuated a language separation policy that undergirded and framed Jenny's sense of herself as a bilingual reader.

While this may be the case, Jenny and Maria acknowledged an important and intimate connection between languages in Jenny's developing identity as a bilingual reader so that languages did not have to compete or be compared to one another. Maria reported that Jenny's teacher said she "loved to read and write" and that she "loves to write stories in both English and Spanish," not showing a preference for one language over the other, and will read whichever book "is more exciting." Maria, in turn, did not interpret Jenny's miscues when reading *Alexander and the Wind-Up Mouse* and *Jack and the Beanstalk* as hindrances or a reflection of difficulties in the process of becoming a bilingual reader. After listening to Jenny read *Jack and the Beanstalk*, Maria reflected on Jenny's reading and said, "Me di cuenta de que tambaleó un poco, pero eso está bien, porque ella está estudiando ambos idiomas" [I noticed that she stumbled a little, but that's okay because she is studying both languages]. She elaborated by saying, "Muy feliz de que élla puede leer en ambos idiomas" [very happy that she can read in both languages] and that she can switch between languages so easily, while proudly showing Jenny's homework notebook and books that she had been reading in school.

When I first met Maria, when Jenny was 5 years old, she explained that she wanted both her children to become bilingual and biliterate. She discussed the great risks that she faced in not only migrating to the United States but also the day-to-day sacrifices she made so that Thomas and later Jenny could attend a dual-language school, traveling one hour each way to take them to school. When Jenny started the dual-language school, Maria decided to get a job at a pizzeria near the school so she could be close to her children. The range and transformation of Jenny's bilingual reading behaviors were the result of the efforts Maria exerted to support her children linguistically and academically.

Lessons Learned From the Biliteracy Manifestations

Built on a revaluing framework, the sessions were organized and designed to take an asset-oriented view of bilingual reading identities to disrupt deficit and narrow perspectives of reading that favor English as the dominant norm for successful reading. Sophie's and Jenny's Profiles, however, show the ways their bilingual reading identities, implemented by collaborative and public processes, were not taken up in the same way. While neither Jenny nor Sophie were considered "struggling" students in their respective schools, their Profiles suggest that the translanguaging context mediated the ways in which their families interpreted their bilingual reading behaviors as successful or not.

The research on how linguistically diverse families support or not support their children's identities and abilities as biliterate individuals has grown over the past 10 years. Early works focused on the social and cultural contexts of reading at home suggest some cultural misalignments within linguistically diverse reading practices. Gregory's (1996) work with linguistically diverse families in the Britain and France showed that parents carry with them their own interpretations and definitions of learning how to read that has cultural origins. Gregory (1996) described how Tony, a young Chinese-speaking boy living in Britain, must "learn to read" before his father allowed him to have books because the memorization of Chinese characters was considered the prerequisite for any type of reading experience by his family. Gregory wrote about the families in her study: "All families view reading as a future investment. Pleasure and satisfaction are seen as the result of hard work and do not belong to the beginning stage of learning to read" (p. 42).

Regardless of the differences in practices and beliefs like those that Gregory described, linguistically diverse families believe that reading in English is a major factor in success in school and for future economic stability (Bus, 2002; Delgado-Gaitan, 1992; Gregory, 1996; Martinez-Roldan & Malave, 2004). They will attempt to support their children's uses of English in reading and writing (Delgado-Gaitan, 1992; Martinez-Roldan & Malave, 2004). At the same time, many families feel that maintaining their heritage language is important to retain membership and connections to their cultural heritages (Gregory, 1996; Gregory et al., 2004). As Sophie's and Jenny's families have illustrated, linguistically diverse families socialize their children into reading practices that are varied and dynamic, as well as influenced by culture, community, and beliefs about reading.

Despite the burgeoning research on translanguaging, the concept is only starting to be applied to language patterns within families. The addition of a translanguaging framework to families has provided mixed findings on how and why family language planning is influenced by ideologies that conflict or align with those of schools (Danjo, 2021; Flores-Ferrán & Suh, 2015; Song, 2016; Wilson, 2020). Applying a translanguaging perspective to the study Japanese and English bilingual families, Danjo (2021) found that bilingual families take a double monolinguistic perspective to language. Through this perspective, language is kept separate by parents so one parent speaks one language. The result is that families promote an ideology of language separation rather than integration. Studying Korean and English bilingual families, Song (2016) and Wilson (2020), however, argue that bilingual families and their children use languages flexibly to promote a translanguaging context within the home. Song found that the families constructed a translanguaging context to support their children's heritage language development. Similarly, Wilson argued that a multilingual ideology filters into families' language practices.

Sophie's and Jenny's families illustrate these types of contradictive findings when identity is added to the diverse ways that families define themselves and their children in the process of becoming bilingual readers. Figures 5.1 and 5.2 are identity maps for Sophie and Jenny illustrating that reading events were windows into the complex and unique ways their identities were constructed. As with any visual representation that attempts to capture a moment in time, identity maps are not designed to depict the entirety or the process of identity construction. Rather, they present a way to compare similarities and differences between two individualized phenomena. These identity maps start with the two reading events that included an English text and a text in Spanish for Jenny and one in Greek for Sophie. Drawing from the unique themes of their families' narratives, the maps visually create linkages among

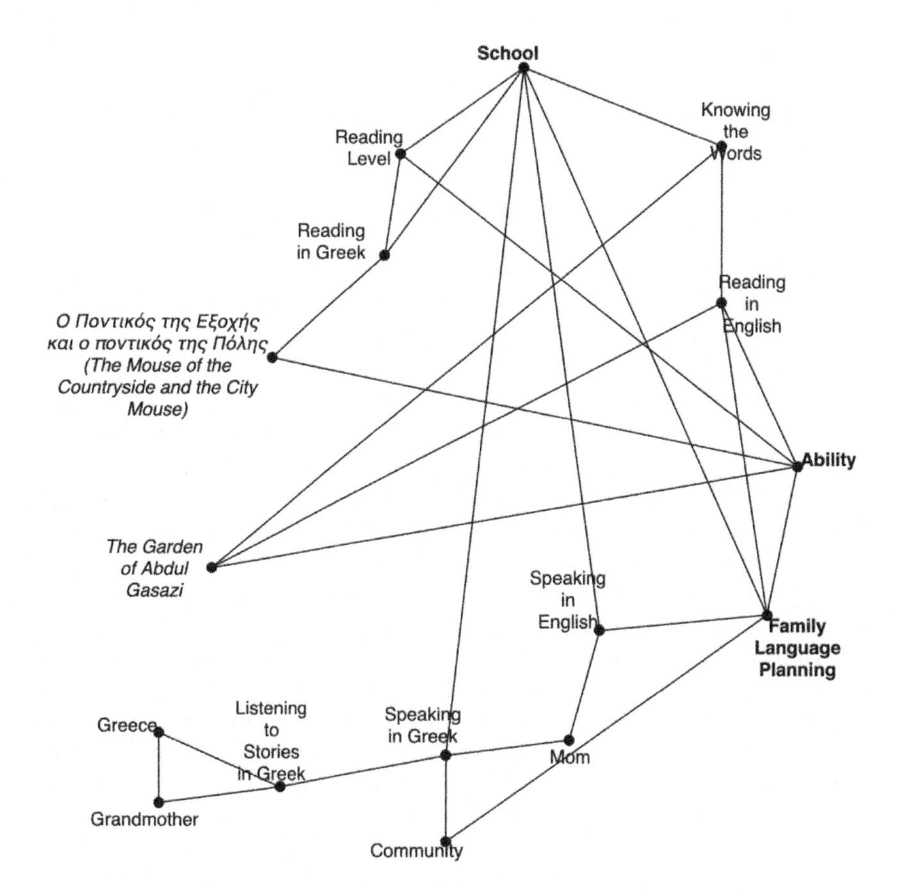

Figure 5.1 Sophie's Identity Map

associated factors to show that, while both readers were considered bilingual readers from bilingual families and attended dual-language schools, the connections among those factors created distinctive identities. The result was that no two maps ended up the same, leading to striking differences between Sophie's and Jenny's maps, even with commonalities between them.

As shown by the conjoining lines, factors linked to school, ability, and family language planning (bolded in the figures) served as sites of identity construction and conflict. Sophie's identity map in Figure 5.1 illustrates a greater degree of contestation within her identity. Speaking in Greek had little connection with reading in Greek and was almost tangential to her experiences in school, barely connected at all to Sophie's and Frances's understanding of what it means to be a capable bilingual reader.

Frances directly described bilingualism as an asset, but ironically reinforced a monoglossic view of language when it came to both speaking and reading across languages. Such a view actualizes monolingualism as the norm, regardless of language modes, and marginalizes the dynamic nature of language, without acknowledging the intricate connections among languages, as noted in a translanguaging context (Flores & Schissel, 2014). Frances interpreted Sophie's miscues from a deficit perspective and the translanguaging context only exacerbated Frances's idea that languages can be compared and measured against each other. In other words, bilingual reading abilities could only be understood in relation to a single reading ability defined by English, reading levels, and other readers of Sophie's age, all linked to school-based conceptions of ability.

While Frances advocated for a dynamic approach to bilingualism, she nonetheless did not have the same approach to biliteracy. In fact, Frances's family language planning ostensibly supported bilingualism by choosing to send Sophie to a private dual-language school, when this, in fact, perpetuated the belief that there can be two distinct ways to be bilingual by separating languages when living in different contexts (United States and Greece). Being biliterate, however, was not valued and supported in the same way. Coming from a financially secure home that allowed for a transnational lifestyle, Sophie's bilingualism was positioned as a commodity. For Frances, English was the language of power and access. As shown in Figure 5.1, English ended up being positioned closely to the ability to achieve a successful academic and career trajectory.

Jenny's identity map in Figure 5.2, in contrast, demonstrates the coherent ways that languages support a more heteroglossic view of bilingualism and biliteracy. This particular view foretells access to linguistic resources within a translanguaging space that supports part of Jenny's bilingual reader identity (Flores & Schissel, 2014). As Figure 5.2 demonstrates, the dynamic and flexible use of languages are represented in how factors related to speaking and reading across languages transverse in complex and interconnected ways. Both Maria and Jenny endorsed movement between languages when reading and retelling stories. Boundaries did not exist. As a result, being a

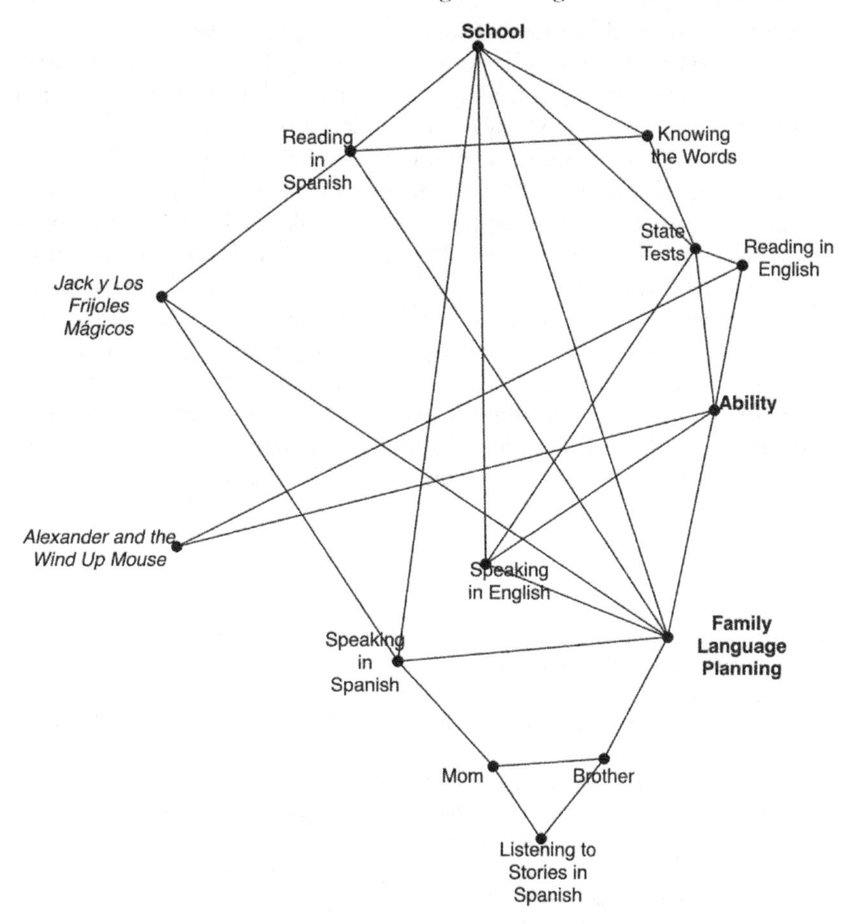

Figure 5.2 Jenny's Identity Map

capable reader meant using all the linguistic resources available to construct and communicate meaning – a centerpiece to becoming a bilingual reader.

Maria's desire to raise her children as bilingual and biliterate was a conscious choice that eventually resulted in her decision to send Thomas and Jenny to a dual-language school rather than their neighborhood school, which offered instruction only in English. By sending her children to a dual-language school, she felt that her home language was valued, consistent with positive societal attitudes, and aligned with school expectations. As such, Maria and Jenny did not see languages as separate and independent of each other. Maria's reflections about Jenny's Spanish miscues as representative of her developing reading proficiencies as she drew from two languages are indicative of bilingualism and biliteracy being part of her long-term aspirations and goals for her children. Figure 5.2 exemplifies how ability, as described through notions of success and struggle, was located in close proximity to Jenny's family's language goals, as they were in Sophie's. Maria's support of Jenny's bilingual reading identity falls in line with other research that highlights how linguistically diverse readers can simultaneously construct positive and multidimensional identities (Park, 2018; Ricklefs, 2020).

The bilingual reading abilities of these two readers, and many others like them, were not defined solely by cognitive abilities. In fact, the identity maps placed school-based factors, like reading levels and state tests, as institutional aspects that construct ability alongside bilingual reading events. While Jenny and Sophie demonstrated effective bilingual reading behaviors as seen through a socio-psycholinguistic perspective to reading that forefronts meaning and reading as a unified language process, these behaviors, as documented through miscue analysis, retelling analyses, and dynamic linguistic behaviors, were interpreted through the lens of dominant narratives controlled by commercial and standardized assessments of what it means to be successful in becoming a reader.

References

Bus, A. (2002). Joint caregiver-child storybook reading: A route to literacy development. In S. Neuman & D. Dickinson (Eds.), *Handbook of early literacy research* (pp. 179–191). Guilford Press.

Danjo, C. (2021). Making sense of family language policy: Japanese-English bilingual children's creative and strategic translingual practices. *International Journal of Bilingual Education and Bilingualism, 24*(2), 292–304.

Delgado-Gaitan, C. (1992). School matters in the Mexican-American home: Socializing children to education. *American Educational Research Journal, 29*(3), 495–513.

Ellis, S., & Smith, V. (2017). Assessment, teacher education and the emergence of professional expertise. *Literacy, 51*(2), 84–93.

Flores, N., & Schissel, J. L. (2014). Dynamic bilingualism as the norm: Envisioning a heteroglossic approach to standards-based reform. *TESOL Quarterly, 48*(3), 454–479.

Flores-Ferrán, N., & Suh, S. (2015). A case study of a Korean-American family's code switching during conflict-related interaction. *Journal of Language Aggression and Conflict, 3*(2), 289–316.

Gee, J. P. (1996). *Social linguistics and literacies: Ideology and discourse* (2nd ed.). Routledge-Falmer.

Gee, J. P. (2004). *An introduction to discourse analysis: Theory and method*. Routledge.

Gregory, E. (1996). *Making sense of a new world: Learning to read in a second language*. Paul Chapman Publishing.

Gregory, E., Long, S., & Volk, D. (2004). A sociocultural approach to learning. In E. Gregory, S. Long, & D. Volk (Eds.), *Many pathways to literacy: Young children learning with siblings, grandparents, peers and communities* (pp. 6–20). Routledge-Falmer.

Heller, M. (1988). Strategic ambiguity: Codeswitching in the management of conflict. In M. Heller (Ed.), *Codeswitching: Anthropological and sociolinguistic perspectives* (pp. 77–96). Mouton de Gruyter.

Holland, D., Lachicotte, W., Skinner, D., & Cain, C. (1998). *Identity and agency in cultural worlds*. Harvard University Press.

Martinez-Roldan, C., & Malave, G. (2004). Language ideologies mediating literacy and identity in bilingual context. *Journal of Early Childhood Literacy, 4*(2), 155–180.

Packer, M. J., & Goicoechea, J. (2000). Sociocultural and constructivist theories of learning: Ontology, not just epistemology. *Educational psychologist, 35*(4), 227–241.

Park, H. (2018). Influences of reading online texts in Korean English language learners' cultural identities. *Journal of Educational Research, 111*(4), 385–97.

Ricklefs, M. A. (2020). Young English learners re-construct their literacy identity. *The International Journal of Learner Diversity and Identities, 27*(1), 15–31.

Rowsell, J., & Pahl, K. (2007). Sedimented identities in texts: Instances of practice. *Reading Research Quarterly, 42*(3), 388–404.

Song, K. (2016). "Okay, I will say in Korean and then in American": Translanguaging practices in bilingual homes. *Journal of Early Childhood Literacy, 16*(1), 84–106.

Taylor, D. (1996). *Toxic literacies: Exposing the injustice of bureaucratic texts.* Greenwood.

Whitmore, K. F., & Meyer, R. J. (2020). Reclaiming manifestations of literacies. In R. J. Meyer & K. F. Whitmore (Eds.), *Reclaiming literacies as meaning kaking: Manifestations of values, identities, relationships, and knowledge* (pp. 1–18). Routledge.

Willis, A. I. (2019). Race, response to intervention, and reading research. *Journal of Literacy Research, 51*(4), 394–419.

Wilson, S. (2020). To mix or not to mix: Parental attitudes towards translanguaging and language management choices. *International Journal of Bilingualism, 25*(1), 58–76.

6 Biographic Biliteracy Profiles: Implications for Creating Culturally Relevant Assessment Practices

When I first envisioned this book, I knew that I had stories to tell, stories that would come together to construct Profiles serving as counternarratives to the many deficit-oriented assessment practices that frame what linguistically diverse readers should know about reading and how they should demonstrate that knowledge. The Profiles of Thomas, Jenny, Sophie, Mai, and Emma illustrate that becoming a bilingual reader is a narrative about life experiences and that texts mediate those experiences by bringing out, valuing, and devaluing certain types of reading and linguistic behaviors.

While I constructed the Profiles with five linguistically diverse readers, these Profiles can be added to the tireless work of others who have, over the years, argued that the assessment practices for linguistically diverse readers ought to be refocused on issues of educational equity and inclusive educational practices (Kinloch et al., 2020; Souto-Manning, 2016; Willis, 2019). In her powerful piece, Willis (2019) described reading research in the late 1960s and 1970s through the lens of critical race theory. Centering language and race as critical to understanding former and current assessment practices of reading, Willis wrote,

> Discarded students included students who were Black and lived in urban areas, Spanish dominant learning to read in English, and low income. The panel's first report was positioned as apolitical, color-blind, and objective, although it applied and extended scientific racism. In reading research, it idealized the U.S. student as English dominant, middle to upper class, with above normal abilities, and White.
>
> (p. 399)

As I was prepared to venture out to tell the stories of these readers in becoming bilingual readers, the unexpected stories of linguistic inequalities and the connections between race and language also came to the surface. These stories have a vital place in understanding both the process of becoming bilingual readers and how educators can resist and replace ideological frames that promote linguistic inequalities in assessment practices with a framework of culturally relevant assessment practices.

DOI: 10.4324/9781003045984-7

Becoming Biliterate Through Being a Bilingual Reader

Centering the Profiles of Thomas, Jenny, Sophie, Mai, and Emma, *Becoming Bilingual Readers* aimed to integrate a translanguaging perspective to support and expand the notion of bilingual reading as a unified, rather than a separate, language process. In other words, translanguaging not only challenged the additive approach to bilingualism but also that bilingual readers are trying to balance two separate linguistic systems (Garcia & Wei, 2014). It also placed the learner and language at the center of assessing linguistically diverse students so that assessment practices are "malleable and designed with an eye toward language of the individual" (Ascenzi-Moreno, 2018, pp. 357–358). With the learner and language at the center, there was a shift in focus away from a singular way of knowing to multicompetence (Cook, 2016). Cook (2016) describes multicompetence as involving the whole mind of linguistically diverse individuals and not naming their languages as first and second. Supported by a translanguaging perspective, multicompetence reinforces the idea that linguistically diverse individuals are different from monolinguals. As such, the reading performance of linguistically diverse readers cannot be compared, measured, or ranked against monolingual readers and speakers of any language.

While translanguaging goes beyond code-switching to capture the full complexity and range of linguistic resources for linguistically diverse readers (Nogueròn-Liu, 2020), code-switching was one way to examine language as a discursive practice and to slow down the linguistic moves within a translanguaging context. Through the analysis of moment-to-moment linguistic shifts, Thomas, Jenny, Sophie, Mai, and Emma demonstrated their multicompetencies as readers. They weaved in and out of language as they engaged in the reading process, retold the stories, and participated in critical reflections of their high-quality miscues. They read books in different languages and writing systems with unique characteristics that precluded a quantitative comparison of their reading performances in English.

Through a socio-psycholinguistic perspective on reading, reading across named written language systems (Greek, Japanese, Spanish, and English) was a transactional and constructive process defined by language cueing systems – syntactic (grammatical), semantic (meaning), and graphophonic – and psycholinguistic strategies. The bilingual reading process was thus a unified reading process in which language separation did not always equate with or support meaning construction. This point falls in line with cautionary comments of other scholars who argue against reducing reading to one perspective dominated and supported by a decoding approach to reading (Compton-Lilly et al., 2020; Nogueròn-Liu, 2020). Nogueròn-Liu (2020) wrote:

> I caution against the implications of discrediting the three-cueing systems and a related assessment tool (miscue analysis using the semantic, graphophonic, and syntactic categories), by explaining how

language-related theories, including translanguaging, can help expand miscue analytic approaches.

(p. S312)

Integrating approaches like translanguaging, code-switching, and miscue analysis can provide a means of creating formative and culturally and linguistically relevant assessment practices for bilingual readers. As scholars remind us, and as these bilingual readers illustrate, an oral reading assessment is just as much a language test as it is a reading one, and language must be taken into account in shaping the reading performances and abilities of bilingual readers (Ascenzi-Moreno, 2018; Noguerón-Liu, 2020; Sanchez et al., 2013).

Table 6.1 outlines how the Reading Miscue Inventory (RMI) can be expanded and adapted to include language-related theories like

Table 6.1 Expanding Miscue Analysis as a Culturally Relevant Reading Assessment Practice

* *Reading Miscue Inventory Components*	*Expanding the Miscue Analysis Approach for Linguistically Diverse Readers*
Burke Reading Interviews	Include questions about reading in each language. Some examples include: *When you are reading in [language] and come to something that you don't know, what do you do? How about when you are reading in [language]?* *Who is a good reader in [language]? How about in [language]? What makes them a good reader?* *How did you learn to read in [language]? How about in [language]?*
Miscue Analysis-Oral Reading	• Before asking readers to read the text, indicate to them that if they come to something that they do not know when reading they should whatever they would do if they were reading alone and in whatever language. • Use diverse texts to listen to, document, and analyze the reading cues and meaning-making strategies. Consider bilingual texts that allow for the fluid movement among languages through code-switching. • Record the reading and explore web and app programs that will translate recorded oral readings. • Acknowledge that accompanying talk can be a window into how readers engage in the reading process. Make notes on the typescript of what readers say when they are reading.
Miscue Analysis-Retelling	• Ask readers to retell the story and, if the retelling seems limited in one language, ask readers to retell it in another language. • If readers are having difficulty with a word or phrase, ask them how they would say it in their other language. • Record the retelling and explore web and app programs that will translate the recorded retellings.

(*Continued*)

Table 6.1 (Continued)

* *Reading Miscue Inventory Components*	*Expanding the Miscue Analysis Approach for Linguistically Diverse Readers*
Knowing the Readers and Perceptions of the Reading Process	• Ask readers to reflect on their miscues and their accompanying talk as windows into their thinking. • Acknowledge the role of diverse texts and languages in constructing readers' performances and abilities. • Challenge English-based text levels as a way to determine or benchmark reading ability. • Connect back to the Burke Reading Inventory (BRI) to find ways that readers' bilingual reading performances support or challenge the information that they provide in the BRI.

* From Goodman et al. (2005)

translanguaging and code-switching to represent a culturally relevant reading assessment. Developing the learning biographies for the Profiles, the Burke Reading Interview (Goodman et al., 2005) helped me get to know the readers and their perceptions of the reading process. Modifying the questions to include languages more explicitly can be insightful and surprising in grasping bilingual readers' views of reading and language as an integrative meaning-making system and to delineate reading as distinctive to each language. By asking questions about learning to read and problem solving, and how they view themselves as readers by language, the bilingual readers in this book provided a framework for me to interpret their bilingual reading behaviors. At times there were tensions and inconsistencies between what the readers reported during the Burke Reading Inventory and what they did when reading, as well as times when their words were supported by their actions.

The backbone of RMI is made up of the oral readings and retellings. RMI recognizes that text mediates the construction of knowledge and that reading performances are key to understanding how ideas of ability can be socially constructed. The readers in this book read text in different written languages and were encouraged to draw upon their linguistic resources when reading and retelling. As a culturally relevant assessment, it is important to ask how and why we select particular texts. I encouraged the readers I worked with to select their own texts, with a few exceptions. In retrospect, it is clear that we were less concerned with certain types of text in the selection process, such as bilingual texts. To this day, I wonder what Jenny's and Thomas's bilingual reading behaviors would have looked like if I had asked them to read bilingual books, for instance, *Mice and Beans* (Ryan, 2001), *Abuela* (Dorros, 1997), *Señorita Mariposa* (Gundersheimer, 2019), or *Martina the Beautiful Cockroach* (Deedy, 2019). Souto-Manning (2016) argued that books allow for "the weaving in and out of languages, providing access while demonstrating code switching" (p. 268). For educators who are monolingual in English, these texts encourage language fluidity and for teachers to participate in meaningful ways. For languages that are not often represented in bilingual books, like Greek, educators can record oral readings and retellings for later translation with apps and online translation sites.

Situating the oral readings and retellings in a translanguaging context promotes the breaking down of artificial boundaries that privilege the language of the text for comprehension. As the Profiles illustrated, understanding and meaning cannot be constrained to a singular linguistic form during the retelling process. At the same time, accompanying talk was part of the formative assessment process and occurred in diverse language forms. As part of the formative assessment process, accompanying talk opened windows into the reading process.

The reading of any text is situated in larger social and cultural contexts and is a product and part of the process of identity construction. As evidenced in some Profiles, the belief that reading performances could be leveled or measured surfaced, although I purposefully did not present the books' levels for these Profiles. In Sophie's Profile, for example, she demonstrated effective reading behaviors when reading in Greek, but neither she nor Frances perceived Sophie's reading ability in Greek to be at the level of her reading in English. For bilingual readers, it is unrealistic and detrimental to a reader's identity to assume that reading across languages will be comparable or equal. Rather, there are ebbs and flows in the kinds of reading performances linguistically diverse readers exhibit, depending on the texts, the context, and the knowledge they bring to the reading event. It is critical that educators acknowledge the role of language and diverse texts in constructing readers' bilingual reading performances and challenge English-based text levels as a way to determine or benchmark reading ability. Instead of measuring readers against levels, it is more productive to meet the readers where they are at as bilingual readers.

As illustrated in the Profiles, becoming bilingual readers necessitates that reading events be situated within a translanguaging context, which also becomes a space for linguistic and identity enactments. By envisioning translanguaging as a context, three main points came to the surface. First, translanguaging as context views linguistic action through the fluidity of language forms that individuals use. Second, through the fluidity and negotiation of language forms, the context was constructed by other people and things (such as texts written in different languages), as well as affording it a temporal nature. The temporal nature of the context evolved from the history and the future aspirations of the readers and their families (Compton-Lilly, 2011). Finally, identity enactments are revealed and configured within a translanguaging context as language forms index certain types of meanings, selves-in-action and sense-of-selves. It was through the translanguaging context that the bilingual readers perceived themselves and provided a lens for how others viewed them as readers.

Identity mapping provided an effective analytic tool to conceptualize the connections between becoming a bilingual reader and the larger concept of becoming biliterate. Biliteracy is more than reading and writing; it is about the intersectional ways that our identities interact to construct an understanding of who we are in relation to the various social spheres in which we participate. Through this view, texts and reading events are sites of identity construction as aspects of our identities intersect within one reading event.

Crenshaw (1991) used the term *intersectionality* "to denote the various ways in which race and gender interact" (p. 1244). Intersectionality has been expanded to include how the multiplicity of our identities inform how we see and interpret the world and our experiences. It helps explore the identities of readers and students, particularly in how we construct counternarratives to the oppressive ways that linguistically and racially diverse readers are positioned (Kinloch et al., 2020). As Kinloch et al. (2020) wrote, "Culturally and linguistically diverse spaces serve as sites that not only support the development and negotiation of identities but also oppress people who resist language normalization" (p. 385). As such, becoming biliterate draws upon bilingual reading, event after event, so that the translanguaging space is one of negotiation and resistance to either becoming biliterate or not.

Comparing Jenny's and Sophie's identity maps illustrates this point by showing how they negotiated their family status, language and literacy aspirations, schooling, and being part of a bilingual family in the process of becoming biliterate. As their Profiles and identity maps exemplify, Jenny, the socioeconomically disadvantaged, racially marginalized reader, was not the struggling reader or from a family that disregarded the importance of school. In fact, it was quite the opposite. Jenny's family developed an ethos that supported her biliteracy while Sophie's family did not.

A Framework for Culturally Relevant Assessment Practices

In Chapter 1, I proposed that Profiles have the potential to be a culturally relevant assessment tool by acting as a formative assessment. As a formative assessment, the bilingual readers' learning biographies, observations of their reading behaviors, and documentation of the reading process (including accompanying talk, retellings, and reflections of readers' miscues), and artifacts that are manifestations of their identities and social worlds form the Profiles. Earlier, I discussed how RMI can be modified to address cultural relevance in assessing reading by expanding how one approaches the documentation and analysis of readers' miscues in a translanguaging context. I will conclude this book with three more pillars to culturally relevant assessment practices – developing a mindset around cultural relevance, acknowledging the connections between race and language, and applying the power of in-the-moment assessment.

Developing a Mindset on the Importance of Cultural Relevance

The first pillar of this framework is developing a mindset, and that mindset begins with recognizing that certain assessment practices, particularly standardized, norm-referenced assessments, can be racially, culturally, and linguistically biased. Researchers have written extensively about the history of education in the United States as a history built on racial and linguistic inequalities (Au, 2010; Garcia, 2009; Noguera, 2016; Spring, 2015). English was the way to Americanize students, and it held a privileged status both in and outside of schools.

The seminal work on educational policy outlined how education for linguistically diverse students has transformed over time through state and federal policies and court cases (e.g., Garcia, 2009; Nieto, 2009). History has shown us that we sometimes take two steps forward and one step back. While bilingual education has been shown to address many diversity issues and inequities in the schooling of linguistically diverse students, states like California and Arizona closed bilingual education programs. California recently passed Proposition 58, which opened up opportunities for bilingual and dual-language education. The families in this book attended schools in New York, where linguistically diverse families and children have access to bilingual education. As Maria described, she sent Thomas to the dual-language school so she could be a part of his education by serving as class mother, helping with homework, and attending parent–teacher conferences without worrying about a translator. She felt a part of the school community, not someone on the fringes. Despite the exhaustive efforts of researchers, policy is not always followed up in practice, and educational policies that keep families like Maria's on the fringes of schooling persist.

While strides have been made, there is still room for growth. Garcia (2009) wrote, "While students in bilingual education learn to function as bilingual individuals and professionals, assessment most often ignores their bilingualism and assesses their abilities and knowledge only, as if they were monolinguals in the language of dominance and power" (p. 367). State standardized testing, particularly high-stakes testing, is an example of the type of assessment practice that has been used to "justify the inequalities among class, racial, ethnic, and linguistic groups" (Garcia & Wei, p. 134). Research on standardized assessments has shown that they possess content biases that reflect one language and culture and not others (Turnbull, 2020) and "psychometric complexities" when assessing and interpreting test results (Sanchez et al., 2013, p. 161). The translation of tests has also raised concerns about validity and reliability because of the ways translations may result in unnatural language (Baker, 2011).

Culturally relevant assessment practices can address issues of educational equity and inclusive assessment practices. These practices place language at the center of assessment. While formative assessment practices can be modified to be culturally relevant, just because one engages in formative assessment practices does not automatically mean that the practice becomes culturally relevant. Likewise, being linguistically diverse is not a requirement for being able to provide culturally relevant assessment practices. Having a culturally relevant mindset means challenging monolingual privileging, which limits what we can learn from and about linguistically diverse readers and how they engage in reading processes and literacy practices. This mindset includes allowing readers to use and perform in multiple languages, even if it makes us comfortable or disrupts how we think we should act as educators or be educators. Disrupting our known beliefs and acknowledging our own privilege are critical steps in creating equitable assessment practices for linguistically diverse students. In this process, confronting explicit and implicit biases, that can frame how one takes up or rejects standardized assessment data to prematurely frame our students as successful or not, are a critical part of the process.

Connections Among Race, Language, and Identity

The connections among race, language, and identity are not new and have been extensively researched and explored (Willis, 2019). Language can index racial categories and cause dichotomies of Self and Other. Shuck (2006) wrote:

> Public discourse surrounding the use of nonstandard varieties of English and non-English languages in the United States, for example, is *racialized* – that is, expressed with indirect or direct reference to racial categories or using rhetorical patterns more often associated with discussions of race and ethnicity, so that an undercurrent of racial distinctions runs through discourse about linguistic differences.
>
> (p. 259)

A statement like "He is Spanish" is an example of how language connects to stereotypes and overly extends identity, language, and nationality, while normalizing the idea that speaking English means being American. Emma's experience in becoming biliterate is another example of how language can imply Otherness and challenge the ways that language positions us. While I have shown the proficient bilingual reading and writing behaviors that Emma demonstrated from a young age in this book and in *Becoming Biliterate*, when she was in kindergarten, she said that she did not want to be "Japanese" anymore. Over the years, and as I revisited Emma's data, I have come to see this statement in different ways. For Emma, not wanting to be Japanese anymore could have been not only a temporary rejection of her bicultural identity but also of her bilingualism.

Revisiting Emma's data has also raised an awareness of the paucity of research on the experiences of Asian Americans in becoming linguistically diverse. Underlying the sometimes invisibility of Asian Americans is the Model Minority Myth (Oluo, 2019; Kim, 2020) that generates stereotypes and universalizes the experiences of Asian American students like Emma. While the socioeconomic statuses of the families in this book range from lower to middle class, and while the schools and resources varied across the families, each reader, in their own way, struggled to make sense of biliteracy against a model of native English speakerism (Kim, 2020).

A common example of trying to conform to a model of native English speakerism is name changing (Thompson, 2006). My mother was no exception when she immigrated to the United States with my father in the early 1970s. To become a naturalized citizen required that she forget her Taiwanese identity encapsulated in the name Ling Tsai and adopt a new identity as Carol, supporting the argument that "an investment in a personal name is an investment in social identity" (Thompson, 2006, p. 190).

Research on binominal identities has opened a rich area of study for understanding the complexities between one's sense of self and assimilation into multiple cultural groups. Thompson (2006) argues that names carry social currency and linguistically diverse groups invest in personal names in order to gain access into social contexts and families will select names that reflect assimilation in multiple cultural and linguistic groups. When Maria named her children, she selected names that sounded quintessentially "American." In naming Emma, her father and I wanted a name that could be represented in English and Japanese and selected a binominal culturally defined name not only for her, but also for her brother Rick. Naming has close connections to identity, family, and culture (Haneda, 2005; Thompson, 2006). Furthermore, as Windt-Val (2012) wrote, "The connection between names and identity does not only affect people. Names and naming also constitute an important part of the work of the building of a nation" (p. 275).

English language privileging in school settings results in parents like my mother and Maria becoming disenfranchised from their children's education. Linguistically diverse parents cannot always engage in school-based practices like helping with homework or reading books at home. Over time, the inequalities only widen as children move up in grades, particularly with state testing and standardized accountability testing becoming continually more dominant in the early grades.

A framework of culturally relevant assessment practices recognizes that there are connections linking race, language, and identity, and any culturally relevant assessment should include diverse ways to collect information that can be used to create a counternarrative to the dominant one that relates race and linguistic diversity with failure. Along these lines, educators should be cautious about using language that positions linguistically diverse students into "static identity categories" (Kinloch et al., 2020, p. 385). In addition, it is critical to acknowledge that there is no ideal student with whom linguistically diverse students can be compared or measured against. Reading levels attached to English texts, for instance, create unhealthy, and sometimes toxic, identities for linguistically diverse readers. Culturally relevant assessment practices use language resources and make language boundaries fluid to reconnect language with success and, hence, support healthy identities between race and language.

In-the-Moment Assessment in Assessing Readers Formatively

Formatively assessing readers can describe reader progress and the process of how and what readers learn. Unlike standardized assessments, formative assessments inform reading instruction (Afflerbach, 2017). Researchers in the literacy field have written extensively about a variety of tools that assist educators in formatively assessing readers, ranging from rubrics to checklists to exit slips. What the field has paid little attention to is the power of assessing, providing feedback, and instructing in-the-moment, particularly for linguistically diverse readers. Formative assessment in reading, whether we listen to readers one-on-one or in small groups, depends heavily on how we respond to readers while they are reading. The Profiles of the bilingual readers in this book show that reading had a purpose over and beyond orally reading the texts for leveling. The reading events were authentic; they were embedded within social contexts and developed around interpersonal relationships among individuals who had vested interests in and particular views of reading.

For linguistically diverse readers, in-the-moment assessment means paying close attention to how we recognize, reject, respond, and support, or fail to support, how readers engage in discursive language practices because educators transmit values and ideologies through their interactions with readers. As Jenny's Profile illustrates, the power of in-the-moment assessment in supporting the translanguaging context was clear. Valuing language flexibility, Livia did not assume that Jenny lacked the vocabulary in English when she tried to find the words that would accurately describe the story. Instead, attention was called to the context and whether it was conducive to disseminating and communicating knowledge so that the knowledge was free-flowing.

To engage in this type of language dynamism in a culturally relevant assessment framework, educators must recognize the biases we bring to the assessment task and how we respond to readers. Questions that can help uncover linguistic biases include the following:

- Do I feel that one language is more important than another for this task?
- Am I privileging one language over another when I respond to the reader?
- What am I assuming about the reader if they switch language forms?
- Am I allowing readers to cross language borders when they are working through reading tasks?

Truthfully addressing these questions requires that educators consider how their identities intersect in complex ways. As I previously described, by doing so, educators can disrupt their unexamined assumptions about language and reading.

There is a body of research illustrating how educators bring their own personal theoretical models of reading when assessing bilingual readers (Ascenzi-Moreno, 2018) and a growing call for educators to be more theoretically flexible when assessing and teaching linguistically diverse readers (Sanchez et al., 2013). Reading accuracy, for instance, may be an impossible goal for novice bilingual readers, such as Mai. Mai's Profile illustrated the complicated relationships between reading accuracy and comprehension, particularly when language was a factor in the reading event.

As such, in-the-moment assessment ought to focus on the meaning- and sense-making processes. The Profiles illustrate that, while all readers made miscues, the miscue patterns were individual to each reader, like a fingerprint, and no two readers used language in the same way to make sense of the texts. Discursive language practices were used to work toward knowledge-building. The translanguaging context was constructed over time as readers changed and evolved in their bilingual reading behaviors, and the other participants recognized the readers' evolving linguistic and reading actions. In-the-moment assessment involved not only reading miscues and retelling content but also developing the readers' bilingual reading identities.

Instead of associating the word *assessment* with terms like *accountability* and *high-stakes testing*, reframing of the word *assessment* should connect to terms like *advocacy* and *equity*. Assessment practices, like those that gave rise to the Profiles, can take a culturally responsive stance towards understanding what linguistically diverse readers know and how they know what they know. Through these practices, we not only uncover how biliteracy is part of readers' personal and family histories but also advocate for, rather than rank and sort, the diverse linguistic knowledge and resources of bilingual readers and their families.

References

Afflerbach, P. (2017). *Understanding and using reading assessment, K-12*. ASCD.

Ascenzi-Moreno, L. (2018). Translanguaging and responsive assessment adaptations: Emergent bilingual readers through the lens of possibility. *Language Arts*, *95*(6), 355–368.

Au, W. (2010). *Unequal by design: High-stakes testing and the standardization of inequality*. Routledge.

Baker, C. (2011). *Foundations of bilingual education and bilingualism*. Multilingual Matters.

Compton-Lilly, C. (2011). Literacy and schooling in one family across time. *Research in the Teaching of English*, *45*(3), 224–251.

Compton-Lilly, C. F., Mitra, A., Guay, M., & Spence, L. K. (2020). A confluence of complexity: Intersections among reading theory, neuroscience, and observations of young readers. *Reading Research Quarterly*, *55*, S185–S195.

Cook, V. (2016). Premises of multi-competence. In V. Cook & L. Wei (Eds.), *The Cambridge handbook of linguistic multi-competence* (pp. 1–25). Cambridge University Press.

Crenshaw, K. (1991). Mapping the margins: Identity politics, intersectionality, and violence against women. *Stanford Law Review*, *43*(6), 1241–1299.

Deedy, C. A. (2019). *Martina the beautiful cockroach*. Peachtree.

Dorros, A. (1997). *Abuela*. Penguin.

Garcia, O. (2009). *Bilingual education in the 21st century: A global perspective*. Wiley-Blackwell.

Garcia, O., & Wei, L. (2014). *Translanguaging: Language, bilingualism, and education*. Palgrave MacMillan.

Goodman, Y., Watson, D., & Burke, C. L. (2005). *Reading miscue inventory: From evaluation to instruction* (2nd ed.). Richard C. Owen.

Gundersheimer, B. (2019). *Señorita Mariposa*. Penguin.

Haneda, M. (2005). Investing in foreign-language writing: A study of two multicultural learners. *Journal of language, identity, and education*, *4*(4), 269–290.

Kim, G. M. (2020). Challenging native speakerism in literacy research and education. *Journal of Literacy Research*, *52*(3), 368–375.

Kinloch, V., Penn, C., & Burkhard, T. (2020). Black Lives Matter: Storying, identities, and counternarratives. *Journal of Literacy Research*, *52*(4), 382–405.

Nieto, D. (2009). A brief history of bilingual education in the United States. *Perspectives on Urban Education*, *6*(1), 61–72.

Noguera, P. A. (2016). Race, education, and the pursuit of equity in the twenty-first century. In P. A. Noguera, J. C. Pierce, & R. Ahram (Eds.), *Race, equity, and education* (pp. 3–23). Springer.

Noguerón-Liu, S. (2020). Expanding the knowledge base in literacy instruction and assessment: Biliteracy and translanguaging perspectives from families, communities, and classrooms. *Reading Research Quarterly*, *55*, S307–S318.

Oluo, I. (2019). *So you want to talk about race*. Hachette Book Group.

Ryan, P. M. (2001). *Rice and beans*. Scholastic.

Sanchez, S. V., Rodriguez, B. J., Soto-Huerta, M. E., Villarreal, F. C., Guerra, N. S., & Flores, B. B. (2013). A case for multidimensional bilingual assessment. *Language Assessment Quarterly*, *10*(2), 160–177.

Shuck, G. (2006). Racializing the nonnative English speaker. *Journal of Language, Identity, and Education*, *5*(4), 259–276.

Souto-Manning, M. (2016). Honoring and building on the rich literacy practices of young bilingual and multilingual learners. *The Reading Teacher*, *70*(3), 263–271.

Spring, J. (2015). *American education: Sociocultural, political, and historical studies in education*. Routledge.

Thompson, R. (2006). Bilingual, bicultural, and binominal identities Personal name investment and the imagination in the lives of Korean Americans. *Journal of Language, Identity, and Education*, *5*(3), 179–208.

Turnbull, B. (2020). Towards new standards in foreign language assessment: Learning from bilingual education. *International Journal of Bilingual Education and Bilingualism*, *23*(4), 488–498.

Willis, A. I. (2019). Race, response to intervention, and reading research. *Journal of Literacy Research*, *51*(4), 394–419.

Windt-Val, B. (2012). Personal names and identity in literary contexts. *Oslo Studies in Language*, *4*(2), 273–284.

Appendix A

Miscue Analysis Classroom Procedure

The classroom procedure analyzes all miscues within the context of the sentence. First, readers orally read the text and the miscues are marked on a prepared typescript using standard miscue markings (see Goodman et al., 2005). The standard miscue markings note substitutions (word, nonword, and complex substitutions where a word-for-word relationship cannot be determined), insertions, omissions, self-corrections, repetitions, and repeated miscues. After the typescript is marked for the miscues, the final produced sentences are coded using the following questions:

1. Syntactic acceptability. The sentence was given a "yes" if the reader's produced sentence was grammatically acceptable.
2. Semantic acceptability. The sentence was given a "yes" if the reader's produced sentence made sense.
3. Meaning change. The sentence was given a "no" if the reader's produced sentence did not change any significant aspect of the story. It was given a "yes" if it did change a significant aspect of the story.

Word-for-word substitutions are coded for graphic similarity. Word-for-word substitutions are marked as having (a) high graphic similarity, (b) some graphic similarity, or (c) no graphic similarity.

After the sentences and word-for-word substitutions are coded, the percentages of yes sentences for syntactic, semantic, and meaning and the percentages for high, some, and no graphic similarity are calculated. These percentages act in conjunction with the retelling data to provide insights into how readers balanced the three cueing systems to read for meaning.

Oral Retellings and Comprehension

Based on the classroom procedure, a retelling is elicited after the reader completes the oral reading. Readers provide an unaided retelling by answering the general question: Can you tell me about what you read? and an aided retelling, which addresses specific follow-up questions. Readers may have various retelling styles ranging from providing detailed, chronological retellings to gist statements that provide overviews of the text.

The retelling scores in the Profiles in this book were calculated through a fiction and nonfiction analytic rubric based on previous miscue studies (Martens et al., 2007; Wilson et al., 2005). The retellings for fictional texts are scored using the following five criteria, or story elements: (a) characters, (b) problem, (c) resolution, (d) events, (e) details, and (f) theme (see Kabuto, 2017). These story elements are rated on a scale of 1 to 4, with 1 being the lowest and 4 being the highest, on the rubric and an average is calculated to provide a holistic view of the retelling. For the nonfiction retellings, the rubric evaluated the retelling based on the following comprehension elements: (a) central purpose/gist, (b) restatement elements, (c) organization, (d) linguistic uses, (e) details, and (f) theme. Similar to the rubric for the fictional text, elements were rated on a scale of 1 to 4, with 1 being the lowest and 4 being the highest, on the rubric. An average is, then, calculated to provide a holistic view of the retelling.

Collaborative and Reflective Conversations

The collaborative conversations are based on Family Retrospective Miscue Analysis (Family RMA; Kabuto, 2009), which incorporates RMA, or retrospective discussions about the readers' oral reading high-quality miscues (Goodman et al., 2014). Family RMA provided me with a starting point and tool for creating a shared space that would allow for discussions about reading with family members.

For Family RMA, the family members who participated in the discussions were shown and listened to preselected oral reading high-quality miscues from their children's oral readings. These are miscues that are grammatically acceptable and meaningful in the sentence and story. After listening to the high-quality miscues, the following questions guided the conversation around the miscues:

1. Can you tell me what you did here?
2. Why do you think you made the miscue?
3. Does the miscue make sense?
4. Did you correct the miscue? Should you have corrected the miscue? Why?
5. Did the miscue affect your understanding of the text?

While the questions helped to guide and initiate the conversation, the ongoing collaborative conversations are not limited to the RMA questions. Rather, the conversation around the readers' bilingual reading behaviors was more fluid and dynamic. While the readers and their families may have answered the questions in the moment, they may have come back to a point or a connection that they made during the Family RMA session later in the conversation or, sometimes, on a different session.

In addition, the collaborative conversations included the readers' and families' perceptions about reading and each other's perceived reading abilities. These conversations were often spontaneous and could have been triggered by an action or memory as the readers tried to make sense of their current experiences through their past educational histories. These spontaneous discussions provided a framework for understanding how readers' biliteracy manifestations had a history and context within the family.

References

Goodman, Y., Martens, P., & Flurkey, A. D. (2014). *The essential RMA: A window into reader's thinking*. Richard C. Owen Publishers.

Goodman, Y., Watson, D., & Burke, C. L. (2005). *Reading miscue inventory: From evaluation to instruction* (2nd ed.). Richard C. Owen Publishers.

Kabuto, B. (2009). Parents and children reading together: The possibilities of Family RMA. *The Reading Teacher, 63*(3), 212–223.

Kabuto, B. (2017). A socio-psycholinguistic perspective on biliteracy: The use of miscue analysis as a culturally relevant assessment tool. *Reading Horizons, 56*(1), 25–44.

Martens, P., Arya, P., Wilson, P., & Jin, L. (2007). Text structures, readings, and retellings: An exploration of two texts. *Literacy Teaching and Learning, 11*(2), 49–64.

Wilson, P., Martens, P., & Arya, P. (2005). Accountability for reading and readers: What the numbers don't tell. *The Reading Teacher, 58*(7), 622–631.

Appendix B

Biographic Biliteracy Profile: Thomas

Learning Biography

Thomas is a sixth-grade student in a public, dual-language school, which he has attended since kindergarten. Thomas lives with his mother, Maria, his father, and his sister Jenny, who is 5 years old and not yet in school. Thomas' family communicates in Spanish at home.

When it was time for Thomas to attend school, Maria was adamant that Thomas continues his education in Spanish while learning English. Thomas's zoned school did not offer a dual-language program and was not rated highly in the school district. Maria said that she would "never allow" Thomas to attend the school. Maria searched out dual-language schools in the district and sent Thomas to another area to attend his current school.

Maria said that reading to her children is important and she read to them every night. Maria compared bedtime reading with her experiences as a child and described how bedtime reading is not part of Ecuadorian culture but she adopted the practice when Thomas's kindergarten teacher recommended it. Thomas said that his mother reading to him was important in learning how to read. Thomas, in turn, reads to his little sister.

Thomas has three dogs and enjoys playing soccer. In school, Thomas likes science class, particularly conducting labs and using microscopes. Thomas said that he reads fiction books, which is his favorite genre.

Thomas expressed confidence in reading diverse texts, and said that he likes to read materials, particularly books, in Spanish or English. Thomas noted he reads more in English than Spanish. He said that if he could spend more time reading, he would like to improve his reading in Spanish because, as Thomas said, "Since I have been doing a lot of English, I would like to learn the language that my grandmother talks . . . Spanish."

Thomas noted that one of the challenges of reading in Spanish is the lack of materials written in Spanish. He said that he mostly reads materials in English at home. To provide her children with more Spanish reading materials, Maria takes them to the public library near Thomas's school on their way home.

Thomas articulated several meaning-centered strategies and differentiated these strategies based on the context. Thomas said that if he comes to a word that he does not know, he will reread the paragraph so he can try to find the meaning of it. If he is unsuccessful, Thomas said that he will go to the computer to try to search the meaning or ask his mom when he is at home. At school, however, Thomas said that he will ask the teacher for the meaning. Observations of Thomas support that he used meaning-centered strategies, as well as a broad range of other strategies when reading.

Observations of a Reader

Thomas conducted six oral readings and retellings: one short story (*Bored Tom*), two Sports Illustrated for Kids articles, and three chapters in the book *Yo, Naomi Leon* (see Table B.1). The oral readings and retellings occurred in a translanguaging context. In some sessions, Thomas read texts written in Spanish, like *Yo, Noami Leon*, and in English, like the articles from Sports Illustrated for Kids. In two of the three oral readings and retelling sessions for *Yo, Noami Leon*, Thomas retold the story in English. There were also sessions in which Thomas discussed his reading patterns and miscues for *Yo, Naomi Leon* in English.

Table B.1 Miscue Analysis Data for Thomas's Profile

Books	*Syntactic Acceptability*	*Semantic Acceptability*	*Meaning Change*	*Graphic Similarity*	*Retelling Score*
English Books					
Bored Tom (Avi, 2008)	Yes: 96%	Yes: 93%	No: 99% Yes: 1%	High: 70% Some: 22% None: 8%	4.0
Small Wonder (Ghosh, 2012)	Yes: 95 %	Yes: 89%	No: 100% Yes: 0%	High: 71% Some: 25% None: 4%	4.0
Good as New (Tapper, 2012)	Yes: 90%	Yes: 79%	No: 100% Yes: 0%	High: 100% Some: 0% None: 0%	3.5
Spanish Books					
Yo, Naomi Leon: Chapter 1 (Ryan, 2005)	Yes: 96%	Yes: 96%	No: 100% Yes: 0%	High: 67% Some: 17% None: 16%	2.25
Yo, Naomi Leon: Chapter 2 (Ryan, 2005)	Yes: 99%	Yes: 98%	No: 100% Yes: 0%	High: 71% Some: 14% None: 15%	4.0
Yo, Naomi Leon: Chapter 3 (Ryan, 2005)	Yes: 99%	Yes: 99%	No: 100% Yes: 0%	High: 67% Some: 0% None: 33%	4.0

When reading, 90% (or more) of the sentences Thomas read were grammatically acceptable. The semantic acceptability of his sentences (i.e., whether they made sense) ranged from 79% when reading *Good as New* to 99% when reading Chapter 3 of *Yo, Naomi Leon*. Thomas demonstrated an understanding of the texts that he read. After reading *Small Wonder*, for instance, Thomas described the story, saying:

> It was talking about what he [Messi] does when he plays soccer. He says what he does [and] about his childhood. When he was little and he practiced and that's why he's a professional football player. Every time he loses, he feels bad for himself. He doesn't scream or stuff like that. He also talks about how he gets prepared for the 2014 World Cup.

Thomas was able to provide specific details like Messi was able to score 50 goals for Barcelona and that he is 5′6 tall.

Based on his retelling scores, Thomas had the most difficulty retelling the first chapter of *Yo, Naomi Leon*, which may be because the first chapter provided general information from the story and introduced some of the main characters. Thomas's retelling scores improved as he read subsequent chapters.

When he read Chapter 3 of *Yo, Naomi Leon*, Thomas retold the chapter as:

> This chapter was about Naomi and Owen and the grandmother talking about Naomi's mother. Naomi noticed that the grandmother would worry about the mother. I think that the grandmother was worried because the mother might take Naomi and Owen away from her to a different place. Since the day that the mother came, the grandmother was not the same. She was different. Her attitude was different.

Table B.2 provides the high-quality miscues that Thomas and I discussed as part of our collaborative and reflective discussions of Thomas' reading. Our collaborative discussions illustrate the ways that Thomas reflected on his reading patterns. He identified the following strategies that he drew upon when he discussed his miscues: meaning, grammar, graphic information, and language experiences.

Meaning and Grammar Strategies

Thomas reflected whether his miscues made sense. When reading *Bored Tom*, Thomas read the sentence, "'But I want to be human,' Tom cried" (Avi, 2008, p. 26) as "'But I want ***to become*** human,' Tom cried". In this example, Thomas substituted *become* for *be*, which did not change the meaning of the sentence or story. When asked about his miscue, Thomas said, "I think it's okay to leave it because if you use *be* or *become* it will make sense. Either way will make sense."

Table B.2 High-Quality Miscues Discussed During Collaborative and Reflective Discussions

Text	*Text Read*	*High-Quality Miscues**	*Thomas' Strategies*
Bored Tom (Avi, 2008)	"But I want to be human," Tom cried (p. 26).	"But I want to ***become*** human," Tom cried.	Meaning Grammar
	So familiar did he become that when Tom went to sleep, Charley slept next to his head on an extra pillow (p. 3).	So familiar did he become that when Tom went to sleep, Charley slept next to ***him (SC*)*** **his** head on ***the*** extra pillow.	Meaning Grammar
Small Wonder (Ghosh, 2012)	In 2010–2011, he scored 50 goals for Barcelona and helped the club win club win titles in the UEFA Champions, League, La Liga, and the FIFA Club World Cup (p. 51).	In ***2010–11***, he scored 50 goals for Barcelona and helped the club win club win titles in the UEFA ***Championships*** League, La Liga, and the FIFA Club World Cup.	Graphic information Familiarity with language
	And with [Barcelona coach Pep] Guadriola, I learned to play tactically, which is what I most needed (p. 51).	And with [Barcelona coach Pep] Guadriola, I learned to play tactically, which is ***most I (SC)*** **what I** most needed.	Meaning Grammar
Good as New (Tapper, 2012)	Stratsburg returned late last season and began to answer those questions when he finished with a 1–1 record and a 1.50 ERA in five starts (p. 43).	Stratsburg returned ***last*** season and began to answer those questions when he finished with a 1–1 record and a 1.50 ERA in five starts.	Meaning Graphic information
	He also suggests finding coaches who emphasize good mechanics to avoid injury (p. 45).	He also suggests finding coaches who ***$empsize (SC)*** **emphasize** good mechanics to avoid injury.	Meaning Language experience
Yo, Naomi Leon, Chapter 1 (Ryan, 2005)	De la alacena empotrada que había sobre mi cabeza, saqué una fuente de plástico donde estaba la última figura que yo misma había tallado en jabon (p. 14). [From the built-in cupboard above me, I pulled out a plastic bowl where my latest soap carving was.]	De la alacena empotrada que había sobre mi cabeza, saqué una fuente de plástico donde **habia** la última figura que yo misma había tallado en jabon. [From the built-in cupboard above me, I pulled out a plastic bowl where my latest soap carving was.]	Meaning

Text	*Text Read*	*High-Quality Miscues**	*Thomas' Strategies*
	Era muy pequeña para recordar por que temblaban, pero la solucíon de abuelita fue mantener mi mente y mis manos ocuoadas (p. 14). [I was too young to remember why they shook, but grandma's decision was to keep my mind and hands busy.]	Era muy pequena para recordar por que ***me*** temblaban, pero la solucíon de abuelita fue mantener mi mente y mis manos ocuoadas. [I was too young to remember why I was shaking, but grandma's decision was to keep my mind and hands busy.]	Meaning Language experience
Yo, Naomi Leon Chapter 2 (Ryan, 2005)	Naomi fue a un psicólogo durante dos años (p. 25). [Naomi went to a psychologist during two years.]	Naomi fue a ***una psicóloga*** durante dos años. [Naomi went to a psychologist during two years.]	Meaning Language experience
	Me prometiste que me dejarías educarlos como es debido interferencias (p. 26). [You promised me that you would allow me to educate them without interferences.]	Me prometiste que me ***dejaras*** educarlos como es debido interferencias. [You promised me that you would allow me to educate them without interferences.]	Graphic information Grammar
Yo, Naomi Leon Chapter 3 (Ryan, 2005)	. . . Fabiola y Bernardo llevaron a varios hombres mexicanos de su ciudad natal que estaban de vista (p. 30). [. . . Fabiola and Bernardo took several Mexican men of his hometown that they were out of sight.]	. . . Fabiola y Bernardo llevaron a varios hombres ***mecánicos*** **(SC) mexicanos** de su ciudad natal que estaban de vista. [. . . Fabiola and Bernardo took several mechanics (SC) Mexican men of his hometown that they were out of sight.]	Graphic information
	Por lo que abuelita sabía, Terri Lynn era tan rebelde que sus abuelos finalmente no quisieron que viviera con ellos (p. 29). [From what grandma knew, Terri Lynn was so rebellious that her grandparents finally did not want that her to live with them.]	***Porque*** **(SC) por lo que** abuelita sabía, Terri Lynn era tan rebelde que sus abuelos finalmente no quisieron que viviera con ellos. [Because (SC) From what grandma knew, Terri Lynn was so rebellious that her grandparents finally did not want that her to live with them.]	Meaning Graphic information

* Miscues are in italics and ***SC*** indicates a self-correction.

When reading *Yo, Naomi Leon*, Thomas read the sentence, "Naomi fue a un psicólogo durante dos años" (Ryan, 2005, p. 25), as "Naomi fue a ***una psicóloga*** durante dos años." In this example, Thomas substituted ***una psicóloga*** for ***un psicólogo***. When listening to his reading of the text, Thomas did not identify the miscue at first and said that he did not catch the miscue because it made sense in the sentence. When asked why he thought he made the miscue, Thomas thought that the psychologist was a woman, which would require the word *una psicóloga*.

Reading for meaning was evident when Thomas reflected on why he self-corrected. When reading Chapter 3 of *Yo, Naomi Leon*, Thomas read the sentence, "Por lo que abuelita sabia, Terri Lynn era tan rebelde que sus abuelos finalmente no quisieron que viviera con ellos" (Ryan, 2005, p. 29) as "***Porque (self-corrected to por lo que)*** abuelita sabia, Terri Lynn era tan rebelde que sus abuelos finalmente no quisieron que viviera con ellos." Thomas substituted ***por lo que*** with ***porque*** and then self-corrected the miscue. When asked why he self-corrected, Thomas said, "Because if I had said, 'porque abuelita', it wouldn't make sense."

Thomas self-corrected a complex miscue that impacted the meaning and grammar of the sentence when reading *Small Wonder*. Thomas read the sentence, "And with [Barcelona coach Pep] Guadriola, I learned to play tactically, which is what I most needed" (Ghosh, 2012, p. 51) as "And with [Barcelona coach Pep] Guadriola, I learned to play tactically, which is ***most I (self-corrected)*** **what I** most needed." In this example, Thomas substituted the phrase "most I" for "what I" and self-corrected to the expected sentence. When asked about his miscue and why he self-corrected it, Thomas said, "I noticed that I skipped a big space and then I reread it. I should have corrected it [because] while I was reading I was listening to myself and noticed that I skipped a part and it didn't make sense."

Graphic Information

Thomas also discussed how he used graphic information in the written text and connected his use of graphic information with other meaning strategies like self-correcting. For instance, when reading Chapter 2 of *Yo, Naomi Leon*, Thomas read the sentence, "Fabiola y Bernardo llevaron a varios hombres mexicanos de su ciudad natal que estaban de vista" (Ryan, 2005, p. 30) as "Fabiola y Bernardo llevaron a varios hombres ***mecánicos (self-corrected)*** **mexicanos** de su ciudad natal que estaban de vista." In this example, Thomas read ***mexicanos*** as ***mecánicos*** and self-corrected. When asked why he thought he made the miscue, Thomas said, "Because after I said, 'mecánicos,' I saw that there was an 'x', so I said, 'mexicanos.'" Thomas noted that both words look alike and that he confused the spellings when he said, "I thought *mexicanos* was spelled [as] /m/ /e/ /j/ /i/ /c/ /a/ /n/ /o/."

Thomas also referenced the graphic information when he explained why he self-corrected his substitution of ***por lo que*** for ***porque*** in the previous example. When asked why he made the miscue, Thomas said, "I think I did that because when I was reading it I didn't see the 'lo' so I said, 'porque,' but then I saw a space there and said, 'por lo que.'"

Thomas also used graphic information to balance his knowledge of language and his experiences with language. Thomas read the sentence, "In 2010–2011, he scored 50 goals for Barcelona and helped the club win club win titles in the UEFA Champions League, La Liga, and the FIFA Club World Cup" (Ghosh, 2012, p. 51) as "In ***2010–11***, he scored 50 goals for Barcelona and helped the club win club win titles in the UEFA ***Championships*** League, La Liga, and the FIFA Club World Cup." In this example, Thomas made two miscues, he read ***2010–2011*** as ***2010–11*** and ***Champions*** as ***Championships***. When asked why he read ***Champions*** as ***Championships***, Thomas said, "Because both words look similar and usually I use *championships*." Thomas noted that the words not only look like but they also represent a similar idea.

Language Experience

Thomas' experience with language was an area that he regularly referenced when engaging in reflective discussions about his miscues. When reading Chapter 1 of *Yo, Naomi Leon* (Ryan, 2005), Thomas read the sentence, "Era muy pequeña para recordar por que temblaban, pero la solucíon de abuelita fue mantener mi mente y mis manos ocuoadas" (p. 14) as "Era muy pequena para recordar por que ***me*** temblaban, pero la solucíon de abuelita fue mantener mi mente y mis manos ocuoadas." When asked why he inserted *me*, Thomas said, "Because usually when I write sentences in Spanish it makes sense like that." Thomas noted that he did not need to self-correct because the insertion made sense.

Thomas expressed that he drew from his language experiences at school. Thomas read the sentence, "He also suggests finding coaches who emphasize good mechanics to avoid injury" (Tapper, 2012, p. 43) as "He also suggests finding coaches who ***$empsize (self-correct)*** **emphasize** good mechanics to avoid injury." When asked why he self-corrected, Thomas said, "Because I've heard my teacher say that word and when I said it didn't sound right so I went back and said the word correctly."

This last example illustrates how Thomas drew from meaning, language experience, and visual information as he read. While the examples were isolated for discussion purposes, there is evidence that Thomas integrated these strategies when he read. This observation suggests that Thomas is reflective and articulate about his reading behaviors when reading linguistically diverse text. He moved seamlessly among the named languages of the text and speakers who were participating in the context to express the range of knowledge he has about his bilingual reading behaviors.

Literacy Manifestations

The construction of Thomas's Profile resulted from interviews with Thomas, his oral readings and retellings with diverse texts, and reflective and collaborative discussions of his miscues. These artifacts, or manifestations, illustrate the complex ways that his reading behaviors were part of the linguistic diversity of the family and school contexts. At the beginning of the sessions, Thomas expressed his confidence in reading diverse texts and within contexts that lacked language barriers and differentiation. The reading data from the miscue analyses support that Thomas was not only comfortable in orally reading and retelling texts presented to him. He was also reflective of his miscues, why he made them, and how the discussions changed him as a reader. In the process, Thomas enacted effective bilingual reading behaviors and was reflective of himself as a bilingual reader.

When asked about reading the diverse texts that were part of the reflective conversations, Thomas responded that he did not feel that he did anything different when reading texts written in Spanish and English. Thomas said, "When I read in English or in Spanish, if I make a mistake I go back to the sentence and make sure that the sentence makes sense." At the end of the sessions, Thomas expressed that he felt himself a good reader and still very comfortable when reading diverse texts. Thomas said, "I feel comfortable reading in both languages." When asked to elaborate, Thomas responded, "Because when I was little, my mom used to read books so I learned like that. At school, I learned how to read in English and Spanish. That made me a better reader."

Having an identity as a bilingual reader and reading with the family at home were themes that threaded through the sessions with Thomas. Not only did Thomas refer back to reading at home with his mother in learning how to read, Thomas also explained how he reads to his younger sister Jenny in either English or Spanish regardless of the written language of the book. Maintaining a sense of being a bilingual reader, Thomas said that he sought out Spanish texts, but the lack of availability was a deterrent in reading these texts. Thomas said, "Most of the books I buy are in English. Sometimes I want to buy a book in Spanish but they are only available in English."

The observations and interviews illustrate how Thomas drew from diverse language forms to develop and support a communicative style. As illustrated by the reflective discussions of his miscues, Thomas moved between the oral and written language forms of the texts to talk about his reading behaviors. Within the translanguaging context, Thomas was able to demonstrate the effective ways that he used reading strategies and understood linguistically diverse texts. At the same time, he drew from the linguistic diversity of the contexts in which he participated.

References

Avi. (2008). Bored Tom. In *Strange happenings: Five tales of transformation* (pp. 1–32). HMH Books for Young Readers.

Ghosh, B. (2012). Small wonder. *Sports Illustrated for Kids, 24*(3), 50–51.

Ryan, P. M. (2005). *Yo, Naomi Leon* (N. Molinero, Trans.). Scholastic en Espanol.

Tapper, C. (2012). Good as new. *Sports Illustrated for Kids, 24*(4), 42–45.

Index

Note: Page numbers in **bold** indicate a table on the corresponding page.

Made in the USA
Coppell, TX
23 January 2024